The Bes

Sussex

Chris & Jackie Parry

Published in the UK by:
Horizon Editions Ltd
Trading as The Horizon Press
The Oaks, Moor Farm Road West, Ashbourne, Derbyshire DE6 1HD
E-mail office@horizonpress.co.uk

1st Edition

ISBN 978-1-84306-443-5

©**Chris and Jackie Parry 2011**

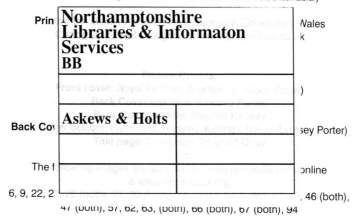

Prin ... Northamptonshire Libraries & Informaton Services BB ... Wales ... k

Front cover: Royal Pavilion, Brighton (Lindsey Porter)

Back Cov ... Askews & Holts ... sey Porter)

The f ... online

6, 9, 22, 2... , 46 (both), 47 (both), 57, 62, 63, (both), 66 (both), 67 (both), 94

South Downs Way, p7: www.nationaltrail.co.uk/Southdowns

All other photographs are supplied by Lindsey Porter

For the sake of clarity, we have decided to the divide this book into chapters based on the ancient divisions of Sussex known as Rapes. In West Sussex, they are: Chichester, Arundel and Bramber; in the East, they are Lewes, Pevensey and Hastings.

DISCLAIMER
While every care has been taken to ensure that the information in this guide is as accurate as possible at the time of publication, the publisher and author accept no responsibility for any loss, injury or inconvenience sustained by anyone using this book. Please note that some attractions may open slightly differently either side of winter. Also that times may vary.

The Best of
Sussex

Chris & Jackie Parry

The Horizon Press

Contents

Welcome to the
Best of Sussex

Top Tips

Sussex is a county of contrasts that excites considerable loyalty, affection and sentimental attachment, evoking even in our post-modern age romantic notions and images about an England that has not quite slipped into history.

Battle of Hastings Site and Battle Abbey

Bignor & Fishbourne Roman Villas

Bluebell Railway

Bodiam Castle

Brighton Pavilion

Chichester Cathedral

Chichester Harbour

Petworth House

Seven Sisters Country Park & Beachy Head

Arundel Castle

Opposite: Arundel Castle
Left: Batemans

Beachy Head and South Downs Way

The lovely Wakehurst Place Gardens

Sussex is the land of the South Saxons, virtually the last of the Anglo-Saxon invaders to convert to Christianity. Its origins in the mists of the Dark Ages relate to the access that its many rivers gave to a largely impenetrable interior, hemmed in against the sea by the great forest of the Weald. Even today, its rivers – the Lavant, the Arun, the Adur, the Ouse, the Cuckmere and the Rother define the county, even as they have shaped its history, development and the rhythms of human life over the centuries. The other well known feature of the Sussex landscape is the chalk hills of the South Downs which stretch from their highest on the Hampshire border in the West, gently descending towards Beachy Head, near Eastbourne, in the East. They present a steep escarpment to the north for most of their length and provide an unbroken series of fine views and lasting impressions.

Although the character of Sussex is defined in the public mind by its distinctive topography and rural image, it is a county of contrasts. Its coast is fringed by a random mixture of progressive resorts, faded grandeur and long stretches of dormitory and retirement development, whereas its hinterland just manages to balance prosperous county towns and rural havens with brash commuter development and the threat of residential conurbations.

The county of Sussex is almost exactly the same area as the bishopric of Chichester. It has, for administrative convenience, been divided into East and West sections since the 12th century, and, despite receiving separate county councils in 1888, remained a single ceremonial county until 1974. It is 78 miles/125km from west to east, with a greatest breadth of 27miles/43km and a coastline of 90miles/144km, enclosing an area of 932,500 ac/377383ha. It is England's thirteenth largest county and its area is roughly split between East (530,000 ac/214491ha) and West Sussex (402,000 ac/162689ha), based on the county towns of Lewes and Chichester respectively.

For the sake of clarity, we have decided to the divide this book into chapters based on the ancient divisions of Sussex known as Rapes. In West Sussex, they are: Chichester, Arundel and Bramber; in the East, they are Lewes, Pevensey and Hastings.

Sussex rapes are divisions of land that vary in size somewhere between a County and a Hundred, similar to the Lathes of Kent and the Ridings of Yorkshire and Lincolnshire. Probably of Anglo-Saxon origin, they were probably sub-divisions of the original South Saxon kingdom that were used to calculate food-rents and military manpower. They were allocated to William the Conqueror's most trusted relatives or barons after 1066, in order to control the routes to the Channel and Normandy and to provide a defensive bridgehead in the event of a successful English insurgency. As such, each rape is centred on a castle, a port, normally with a navigable river, and each was held by a single tenant-in-chief, who appointed the sheriff (no royal sheriffs were appointed in Sussex until the 12th century).

We trust that, apart from being more interesting for the reader, this arrangement avoids artificial boundaries based on modern, sterile administrative conventions and gives a better indication of how each part of the county developed – and reflected - an individual sense of identity over the centuries.

Overall, the book has been written with the visitor who wants to understand and experience the best that Sussex has to offer in terms of scenery, historic sites and attractions. It neither seeks nor aspires to be a comprehensive guide to everything that might appeal to everyone and contains only those features and places that we have come to treasure and which we judge might be of interest to others. Discerning visitors will find their own favourite parts of this endlessly fascinating and varied county. We hope that our selection represents an introductory range of opportunities for the visitor to explore and appreciate the distinctive character, rich history and secret places of this ancient land of the South Saxons.

The Basics – Some things worth knowing about Sussex

The Weather

South East England combines the highest average daytime temperatures found in the British Isles with the highest sunshine averages on the British mainland. Rainfall is heaviest on the South Downs with 950 mm (37 inches) of rainfall.

The weather of the coast is strongly affected by the sea, which, because it tends to warm more slowly than the land can result in cooler temperatures on the coast than inland during the summer. At this time, rainfall is mainly from thunderstorms. In autumn, the coast sometimes has higher temperatures, but thundery showers are more frequent. Overall, the coast has consistently more sunshine than the inland areas, as sea breezes, blowing onto land tend to clear cloud from the coast and up over the Downs.

The South Downs

The South Downs are chalk hills that run for about 70 miles (112 km) from east to west and seven miles (11.2 km) wide, north to south. Both North and South Downs meet at the river valley of the Meon at the Wessex Downs, just inside the Hampshire border. Four rivers cut through the Downs: the Arun, Adur, Ouse and Cuckmere. At 270 m (886 ft), the highest point on the South Downs is Butser Hill, just south of Petersfield, in Hampshire. There are 741 Scheduled Ancient Monuments in the South Downs and the route of the South Downs Way has been used for travel for over 8,000 years, since the Middle Stone Age.

The South Downs National Park

The South Downs National Park became the tenth National Park designated in England in April 2010 and includes an area of 627 sq miles (1600 square km), 67% of which is in Sussex. It stretches for 90 miles (140

*Country Fair at **Buchan Country Park**, Crawley*

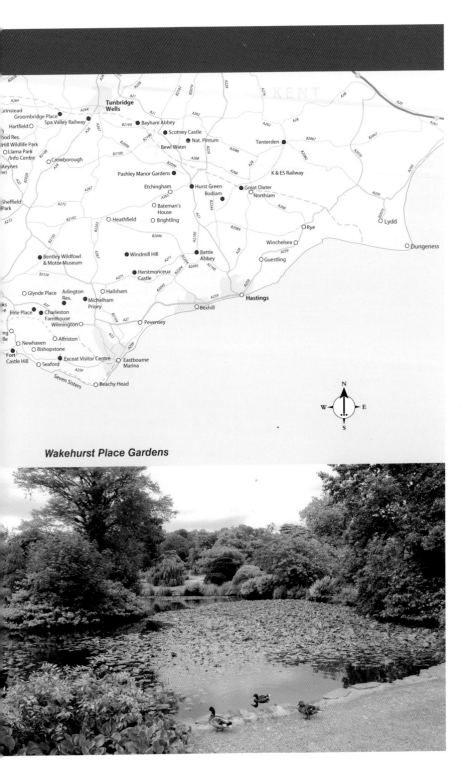

Wakehurst Place Gardens

km), from St Catherine's Hill near Winchester in Hampshire in the west to Beachy Head, near Eastbourne in East Sussex in the east. The southern boundary of the park lies a few miles inland along most of its length, excluding the coastal towns and cities of Portsmouth, Chichester, Bognor Regis, Littlehampton, Worthing and Brighton, but including the towns of Petersfield, Liss, Midhurst and Petworth in the Western Weald, and Arundel and Lewes. It takes in two Areas of Outstanding Natural Beauty (AONB) – East Hampshire and the Sussex Downs – and the South Downs Way.

The Park's operating authority's objectives are "to conserve and enhance the natural beauty, wildlife and cultural heritage of the area" and "to promote opportunities for the understanding and enjoyment of the Park's special qualities by the public", together with a duty to "seek to foster the economic and social well-being of the communities living within the National Park".

The South Downs Way

This major long distance path is available for walking, cycling and riding along almost its entire 100 miles/160 km length from Winchester in Hampshire to Beachy Head, near Eastbourne.

The Weald

The Weald is a geologically defined area of topography in the south-east of England. It has been said to resemble a rough triangle lying on its side whose point stretches across most of Sussex towards Hampshire and includes parts of Kent and Surrey, with its base resting on the coast between Beachy Head and Folkestone. Formed geologically by the erosion of layers of a dome of land between the North and South Downs, the High Weald in the centre comprises exposed sandstone ridges, while the Low Weald features clay valleys, with a Greensand Ridge surrounding its north and west sides and including its highest points.

The huge forest of the Weald in Anglo-Saxon times has been calculated to have been about 90 miles wide and 30 miles deep, taking in most of Sussex to the north of the Downs and some of the adjacent counties as well. Since then, it has been extensively cleared, firstly in the medieval period for agriculture, but later for iron-working, glass manufacture and ship-building. It took 30 acres of forest to build the Tudor warship, the Mary Rose, and 2,000 mature oaks to build HMS Victory. Even so, about a tenth of the county is wooded today and Sussex is the second most wooded county in England. The most extensive sections of forest remaining are Ashdown and St Leonard's, both of which are in the centre of the county.

In Roman and Anglo-Saxon times, the area was densely and, in places, impenetrably wooded and home to extensive iron workings and scattered settlements. It was known as the Andredes weald, "the forest of Andred", a name derived from Anderida - the Roman fort at

Pevensey – and weald – the Old English word for forest. Today, the High Weald Area of Outstanding Natural Beauty includes the ancient Ashdown Forest, whose heaths and woods are punctuated by sandstone outcrops, streams and steep ravines, with farms and villages often linked by sunken lanes and paths.

The extensive forest, plentiful supply of water and access to ore meant that the Weald was heavily involved in the production of iron, especially through the use of charcoal for reducing the ore. From prehistoric times, iron-working has taken place in the Weald, particularly during Roman, Medieval and early modern periods. The first iron cannon made in a single piece was cast in 1543, but the excessive exploitation of the timber led to restrictions on its use. This, coupled with the widespread use of coke extracted from coal saw the production of iron move away to coal-rich areas, although cannon were still being made as late as the 1780s in Robertsbridge, Ashburnham and Fernhurst. The numerous 'hammer' and 'furnace' ponds are reminders of this once thriving industry.

Stane Street

Stane Street is the modern name for a 56 miles/90km long Roman road that linked London to Chichester. Coin finds on the route of the road indicate that it was in use at least by 60-70 AD and was the only significant **Roman Road** in Sussex. Running straight from London Bridge, the road only varies to avoid substantial gradients and attempts to stay on chalk rather than clay. Stane is the old English version of stone and was used to emphasise a paved Roman road rather than a track. The route has several branch lines that go into the Weald, towards agricultural areas and along the south coast.

The route was served by posting stations at intervals where horses could be changed and travellers rested for the night, the Roman equivalent of motorway services. Two are known, at Alfoldean and Hardham, with two others probably at Merton Priory and Dorking. An excavation at Alfoldean produced the remains of a two storey mansio (or motel) built around a courtyard, with other buildings, within a 2.5 hectares/6ha site fortified by ramparts and ditches 4m wide and as deep which were dated by pottery finds to around 90 AD. The ditches were filled in by the mid-third century. The best part of the road today is in Eartham Woods (north-east of Chichester) where the Monarch's Way long-distance path follows the route and the flint surface and boundary ditches on each side can be still be seen.

Churches

Sussex is remarkably rich in the quality and antiquity of its churches, most of which date from Saxon and Norman times, with many retaining their original features. The visitor will notice that almost every village or town in the county has a church of some distinction and it would be easy to make this book a gazetteer

Bodiam Castle

Herstmonceux Castle

*The **Royal Pavilion**, Brighton*

of ecclesiastical architecture. We have simply highlighted the churches that have impressed us most, but the visitor might wish to reflect that almost any village and most towns in Sussex are likely to have a church of interest.

Another feature of Sussex that the visitor will notice is the high incidence of place-names ending in – ing, such as Lancing, Sompting and Hastings. This ending derives from the Saxon ending – ingas, which means the people, tribe or clan of someone. Thus, Hastings is the people of Hasta or a similar sounding chieftain from the Saxon period.

The Cinque Ports

In the 11th century, Edward the Confessor granted the Kentish towns of Sandwich, Dover and New Romney certain privileges in return for providing ships and seamen for the royal service, especially in defending the eastern end of the English Channel from pirates, assorted Scandinavian marauders and invasion. **Hastings** and **Hythe** were added to form the 'five ports' and **Rye** and **Winchelsea** joined the confederation as 'Ancient Towns'. Other smaller towns became 'limbs' of the major ports – in Sussex, **Pevensey** and **Seaford** were attached to Hastings – and shared their privileges and obligations.

Throughout the medieval period, the ports received privileges relating to trading concessions and freedom from royal and other jurisdictions while providing the backbone of fleets used by, or in conjunction with, royal ships. They were especially useful in wars against the French, in resisting raids and in maintaining trading links with Flanders and France. The powerful leading citizens of the Cinque Ports were known as 'barons' and each major town sent two Members to Parliament.

Once climate change caused the sea to desert their harbours and the costs and technical requirements of the Tudor, and particularly the Elizabethan, Navy became prohibitive, the role and importance of the Cinque Ports declined rapidly at the end of the medieval period. Continuing as 'rotten boroughs' until the Great Reform Act of 1832, most of their privileges were abolished in 1855, but the confederation is still headed today, for ceremonial and remaining administrative purposes, by the Lord Warden, whose official residence is at Walmer Castle, in Kent.

The Seven Good Things of Sussex

Interestingly, given Sussex people's dependence in the past on the sea and rivers, the seven 'good things' are:

Pulborough eel, Selsey cockle, Chichester lobster, Rye herring, Arundel mullet, Amberley trout and Bourne wheatear.

Early Sussex

It is thought that Sussex was sparsely populated in Roman times. The only significant settlement was the city of Noviomagus (Chichester), whose foundation seems to have been determined by its proximity to the tribal heartlands of the British ally of Rome, King Cogidubnus, and the sea access provided by Chichester harbour. It is not surprising that the most important Roman Road in Sussex (Stane Street) ran from London to Chichester and that two others, running to Portslade and to the vicinity of Lewes, seem simply to have been constructed to access and exploit the agricultural and iron-working areas of the Weald.

Towards the end of the 3rd century, there were increasing numbers of attacks from the sea on communities on the Channel coast by pirates and raiders of Germanic origin, including Saxons, Frisians and Franks. The coast of Sussex, with its many navigable rivers giving access deep into the interior, was especially vulnerable and about this time, there is evidence for the destruction of villa sites and the building of town walls around **Chichester**. The Roman response was to build a chain of fortresses from the Wash round to Portchester in Hampshire, which combined with a powerful fleet was designed to deal with the security problem. One of these fortresses was at Pevensey, with another possibly underlying the castle at **Lewes** and the next in the chain at Lympne in Kent, perhaps reflecting the sparsely populated demographics of the area. The overall system came to be known as the Saxon Shore and its commander, the Count of the Saxon Shore.

Over the course of the 4th century the pressure from raiding became greater and the Roman imperial power to intervene weakened, owing to pressure on the frontiers elsewhere. Progressively after about 410, the British were left to defend themselves at a time when Germanic war-bands and their populations were looking to seize land and settle Britain. The Anglo-Saxon Chronicle says that in, 477, 'Aelle came, with his three sons, Cymen, Wlencing and Cissa in three ships at the place called Cymenes Ora (probably Selsey) and there they slew many Britons and drove some to flight in the wood that is called Andredes leag (the Weald)'. After years of warfare, this led to a total massacre of the Britons at Pevensey Roman fort in 491 and, at the same time as rapidly increasing Saxon immigration, it seems that the kingdom of the South Saxons was finally established, to the extent that Aelle was hailed by other kings as bretwalda, or Lord of Britain. Despite St Augustine's mission to Kent in 597, the South Saxons remained defiantly pagan until the arrival of Wilfrid. Even then, they did not like him initially – he had a reputation for being fairly confrontational and assertive – and he had to flee. He had more success on his return between 680-1, partly because of his ability to perform magic tricks/miracles, all faithfully reported by his biographer. However, the real key to his success this time was the support of the Aethelwealh,

The Stade, Hastings, where boats
still pull up on the beach

Batemans, the home of Rudyard Kipling

the King of the South Saxons, who probably saw Christianity as a means of protecting himself against his powerful Christian neighbours. Wilfrid was only able to establish a see in 705.

This is because, during the ongoing power struggles and wars between the seven main Anglo-Saxon kingdoms at this time, the South Saxons were struggling to maintain their independent status, in the face of more powerful or more numerous opponents. For the rest of the Anglo-Saxon period, the South Saxons were subjected and absorbed by the West Saxon kings. The county suffered heavily as a result of Viking raiding in the 8th and 9th centuries, finally coming under the re-asserted national kingship of Alfred and his successors. Under Edward the Confessor (1042-66), Sussex was controlled by the powerful Godwin clan, counterbalanced by numerous royal grants to Norman monasteries and religious figures. From this point, Sussex takes centre stage in the struggle between Harold Godwinson and William Duke of Normandy for the succession to the throne of England. On the **Bayeux Tapestry**, Harold sails from Bosham on his ill-fated voyage which ends in capture, William lands at Pevensey, builds a castle and devastates the surrounding countryside and the historic battle is fought at Senlac Hill. To secure his lines of communication back to Normandy and to provide a secure bridgehead in case of a successful English fight-back, William granted blocks of land

to his closest relations and most important followers. These were called rapes, originally five defined districts of Sussex, exclusive to the county, established in late Saxon times and possibly associated with earlier taxation arrangements or military obligations. **Arundel** went to Roger de Montgomery, **Bramber** to William de Braose, **Lewes** to William de Warenne, **Pevensey** to Robert, Count of Mortain and **Hastings** to Robert, Count of Eu. All built a castle and developed a port on the individual river associated with their rape. **Chichester** became a sixth rape when Roger de Montgomery built a castle there and the cathedral was transferred from Selsey to Chichester in 1075.

After the Norman Conquest, Sussex became very much involved in the affairs of the Norman and Angevin kings and their cross-Channel rights and dynastic ambitions. Not surprisingly, the men of Sussex were active in trade and warfare, most notably through the confederation of the Cinque Ports. At the same time, the inhabitants of the coastal region had to deal with the effects of climate change and the perverse action of the sea in markedly changing coastlines and alternately inundating and deserting ports and settlements seemingly at random. Inland, the landowners and inhabitants of Sussex were able to thrive through the production of iron, timber and agricultural output. This pattern continued into the later Middle Ages, interspersed with lethal cross-Channel during the frequent wars between the kings of England and France, most notably during the Hundred Years War.

At this point, the people of Sussex enter the mainstream of English history and their story becomes the common experience of the rest of the country. In all events and decisions, riots and rebellions, taxes and evasions, defensive and offensive wars, it was by now scarcely possible to separate the local from the national and it is now time to turn aside from the good people of Sussex past and concentrate on what is best about their county today.

1. The Rape of Chichester

Hard up against the border with Hampshire, the rape of Chichester was originally part of the rape of Arundel, but was formed by Robert de Montgomery in order to increase his revenues and power base. The South Downs chalk escarpment runs across to the north of Chichester itself, while the northern section is part of the Western Weald, a mix of sandstone ridges and low lying clay, culminating in Black Down, the highest point in Sussex at 919ft/280m. Although, further south, the irregular shape of Chichester Harbour penetrates deep into the area to the south west and the sea seems ever present, the eye is constantly drawn to a northern horizon dominated by the imposing line of chalk grassland. Here, the cathedral city and administrative centre of West Sussex, Chichester is the oldest inhabited civic settlement in Sussex and generally sets the tone for its prosperous area.

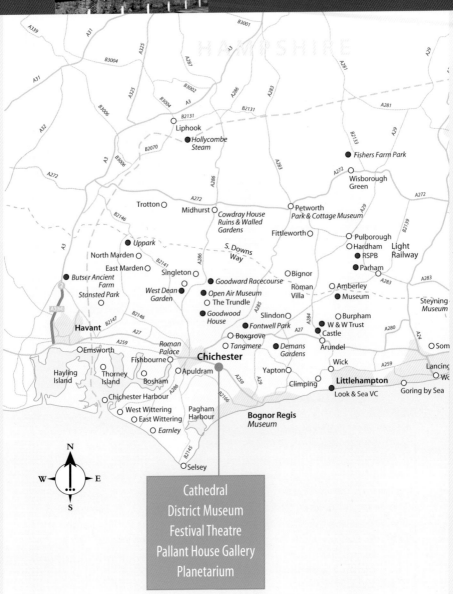

HAMPSHIRE

Liphook

● *Hollycombe Steam*

● *Fishers Farm Park*

Wisborough Green

Trotton ○   Midhurst ○   *Cowdray House Ruins & Walled Gardens*   ○ Petworth *Park & Cottage Museum*

Fittleworth ○   ○ Pulborough
○ Hardham
● RSPB   Light Railway

● *Uppark*   *S. Downs Way*

North Marden ○   ● Parham

East Marden ○   Singleton ○   ● Bignor   ○ Amberley
Roman Villa   ● Museum

● *Butser Ancient Farm*
Stansted Park ○   *West Dean Garden*   ● *Goodward Racecourse*
● *Open Air Museum*
○ *The Trundle*
● *Goodwood House*   Slindon ○   ○ Burpham
● W & W Trust

Steyning Museum

Havant   ● *Fontwell Park*   Castle
○ Boxgrove   ○ Tangmere   ● *Demans Gardens*   Arundel ●

Emsworth ○   *Roman Palace*   Wick

Fishbourne   **Chichester** ●   Yapton ○

Hayling Island   Thorney Island   Bosham   ○ Apuldram   Climbing ○   Littlehampton
Look & Sea VC   Goring by Sea ○

Lancing
○ W

Chichester Harbour

West Wittering ○   Pagham Harbour
East Wittering ○

○ Earnley   **Bognor Regis** *Museum*

N
W   E
S

○ Selsey

Cathedral
District Museum
Festival Theatre
Pallant House Gallery
Planetarium

Chichester

Chichester is the county town of West Sussex. The settlement there dates from before Roman times and was the 'new city on the plain' (Noviomagus) occupied by the people who had previously occupied the hill fort known as the Trundle, near **Goodwood**. The local king at the time of the Roman invasion of 43 was Cogidubnus and he is believed to have been a notable ally before and during the assault and subsequent operations. His loyalty and collaborative stance were rewarded with the status of 'king and imperial legate' and the wealth and power that allowed him and his family to build the magnificent palace at nearby **Fishbourne**.

By the time that the South Saxons came to settle, the city that had been walled in about 200 AD was already in serious decline and its buildings in an advanced state of disrepair. It continued to be occupied during Saxon times, but the arrival of the Normans led to its rise again as a city. Roger de Montgomery built a castle in the north east quadrant, whose motte can still be seen today, and the cathedral of the South Saxons was moved from Selsey. During the medieval period, the town and port grew rapidly through the trade in wool and cloth, as well as cereal and agricultural products. It suffered considerable damage when besieged and captured by the Parliamentarian forces of Sir William Waller in 1642, but recovered to be a prosperous Georgian city, with

Worth Visiting

Pallant House, built in 1712 for a local wine-merchant, who had a look-out installed on the roof to watch for his ships arriving. It now houses a popular art gallery, which displays, both modern and traditional art, most notably the collection of Dean Hussey.

Chichester District Museum is in an 18th century corn store and has exhibits and exhibitions about local history, geology and archaeology.

In **Priory Park**, the remains of the castle motte can be seen, as well as the chancel of a chapel that used to be part of Greyfriars' Priory. It was a shire hall after the Dissolution and William Blake was tried here for sedition in 1804.

The Festival Theatre, just to the north of the walls, built in 1962 under its first director, Sir Laurence Olivier, is a popular centre for theatre and the performing arts.Despite the occasional whiff of pretentiousness among its clientele, it runs a notable summer season of stage productions in its main theatre and in the smaller Minerva, which always attract actors and directors of international repute. Out of season, there is a regular programme of performances by all types of entertainers which are suitable for a range of audiences, young and old.

The South Downs Planetarium and Science Centre permits visitors to see weather pictures from satellites, images from the Hubble telescope and other space-related objects of interest in a special 100-seat building.

many fine buildings dating from that period.

This charming city of brick and flint today retains a large proportion of its (Roman and Medieval) walled circuit, which makes for a very agreeable walk (one and a half miles), and the pattern of its irregular streets closely reflects its original plan, with the four main Roman streets converging on a very fine, eight-sided Market Cross, built in 1501, with a bust of Charles I, a belfry and four clock faces added in the 17th and 18th centuries. The city is best explored on foot and in detail, especially around the many side streets and among some notable examples of English domestic architecture that hold themselves aloof and apart from the bustling, but contained retail element of the city. There are good opportunities for shopping with many quality outlets represented.

Chichester Cathedral

The original cathedral of the South Saxons, built by St Wilfrid in 681, was at Selsey, but the seat of the bishop was transferred to Chichester in 1075. This reflected the Norman tendency – and preference – to site baronial and ecclesiastical power together, and the new cathedral was built of Caen stone, and consecrated in 1108, in the south west quadrant of the Roman city. Unfortunately, a major fire in 1187 burned most of the town and gutted the cathedral, resulting in a re-building by 1199. In the 13th century, the crossing tower was added and a Norman apsidal

Worth A Glance

The Council House in North Street which was built in 1731, with an Assembly Room added in 1783.

Earnley Butterflies & Gardens provides three different experiences, which will amuse children mostly. There are tropical butterflies and exotic birds, alongside a maze of theme gardens, as well as Noah's Ark animal and reptile rescue centre and Rejectamenta, a nostalgic look back at Britain in the 20th century.

St Mary's Hospital in St Martin's Square dates from about 1269 and was built to provide refuge for 13 elderly, deserving people as well as the sick and poor travellers. The Infirmary Hall is joined to a chapel so that the sick could hear Mass while in bed and there are 24 stalls with carved misericords.

eastern end converted into a Lady Chapel. At the same time, chapels added on each side of the nave, forming the double aisles that remain today. The spire was completed in about 1402, just before the detached bell tower, which was placed to the north of the west end to avoid subsidence.

Owing to the water table and ancient river courses, Chichester has always had a problem with subsidence. The south-west tower of the facade collapsed in 1210 and was rebuilt, while its north-west partner collapsed in 1635 and was not rebuilt until 1901. The

Chichester Market Cross

Chichester Harbour

Traditionally thatched cottages in Selsey

spire was repaired in the 17th century by **Sir Christopher Wren**, and, having survived a lightning strike in 1721, collapsed inwards in 1861. As a result of a fund that reached £48,000, including a contribution from Queen Victoria, an 270ft/82m replacement was rebuilt by Sir George Gilbert Scott (Albert Memorial and St Pancras Station) five years later.

From 1262, the cathedral contained the shrine of Richard de la Wyche, (bishop 1245 to 1253), or Saint Richard of Chichester, but this was destroyed in 1538. Further damage was sustained at the hands of Parliamentary troops during the Civil War and by German bombing in 1943.

A notable figure in the cathedral's recent history was Walter Hussey (Dean, 1955-77), who was an active commissioner of contemporary artists and composers, including Sutherland, Piper and Chagall and the composer Leonard Bernstein ('Chichester Psalms' (1965), which were set to the original Hebrew. Kenneth Clark said that he was 'the last great patron of art in the Church of England.' Hussey also acquired many items himself and gave his extensive art collection in exchange for the refurbishment of Pallant House as an art gallery.

The cathedral, which is easily accessible on West Street, is light, airy and quiet. It contains several features worthy of notice:

The detached bell tower (built in 1436 and the only one surviving in England) has eight bells, the oldest of which was cast in 1583.

Outside the west front, with its twin towers, there is a (2002) statue of St Richard by the Royal Sculptor, Philip Jackson (born 1944).

The Norman arcades and triforium of the nave and the later Gothic clerestory and ribbed vaulting, with their Purbeck marble shafts.

The south aisle of the choir has limestone reliefs in the Saxon style of about 1125 portraying the Raising of Lazarus and the Arrival of Christ at Bethany. Here also can be seen an exposed fragment of Roman mosaic, well below floor level. The notable modern art, including a tapestry of the four elements, the Trinity and the four evangelists by John Piper, Noli me Tangere by Graham Sutherland and a red window of David with his harp by Marc Chagall.

The Lady Chapel, at the east end

In the north aisle, the tomb of Richard Fitzalan, Earl of Arundel, executed by Richard II in 1397, and his wife, the subject of Philip Larkin's poem the Arundel Tomb.

Several interesting tombs and memorials, including one to the politician, William Huskisson, the first man to be killed by a train, Bishop Luffa (maybe), the founder, in the Lady Chapel, the ashes of the composer Gustav Holst (north transept) and the odd bishop or two.

The 15th century cloister, which only has a southern half and a barrel-vaulted wooden roof, enclosing a burial ground known as the Paradise. It also leads to a very welcoming café and tea-room.

The cloister also leads to St Richard's Walk and the Cathedral Close which contains many attractive buildings, which can be seen at close quarters on a walk round the south side of the cathedral and through Canon Gate into South Street. The Close is a tight group of attractive buildings, including medieval survivals forming parts of later buildings and a maze of walled gardens. Notable buildings in passing are the Bishop's Palace, the 18th century Deanery and the 14th century Vicars' Hall. The delightful Bishop's Garden can be viewed and accessed from the south wall walk. It should be noted that the 15th century Chapter House and Library are not usually accessible to the general public.

Out and About

Chichester Harbour is a natural harbour (actually, a ria, or drowned river valley) of about 27sq miles/70sq ha of navigable, tidal water and shallow water habitats just to the south-west of the city. Its largely unspoilt coastline comprises settled villages and arable farmland, together with extensive boatyard, marina and tourism facilities. With its inlets and settled villages, as well as access to the Solent, it is a very popular yachting area, with several well-equipped marinas and sailing opportunities for all ages and abilities. It is equally well-suited for walking, bird-watching and exploring, ideally on foot around the creeks, on top of the sea walls and along the sign-posted footpaths. There are impressive views in all directions.

The harbour is also an Area of Outstanding Natural Beauty and is of national and international importance for nature conservation and as a Site of Special Scientific Interest (SSSI) and Special Area of Conservation. Its wetlands and tidal marshes are home to a wide variety of resident and migratory species.

Thorney Island is a peninsula that extends into Chichester Harbour with a footpath, part of the Sussex Border Path, running around its edge. The southern part of the island, which was a busy RAF airfield from 1938 up until the 1960s, is now home to an operational Royal Artillery regiment. Walkers can access the whole path by providing identity details at the security gates and must keep to the footpath marked by yellow posts. On the eastern side of the island is the unspoilt Early English (medieval) church of St Nicholas, while to the south, a sandbank leads to Pilsey Island, an RSPB nature reserve. Its neighbouring peninsula to the east, Chidham, is ideal for a walk that combines coastal and rural elements, with a first-class pub to boot (The Old House at Home).

The picturesque and much-visited village of **Bosham** lies at the head of a tidal creek and, with its cluster of former fishermen's cottages and Blue Anchor pub, is a popular centre for boating and yachting. From the 8th century, it was an important port, which later appeared and was named on the Bayeux Tapestry as the point of departure for Harold's ill-fated voyage that led to his detention by William of Normandy in 1064. Its church is a jumble of Saxon and medieval elements and various unsubstantiated claims have been made for the people likely to have been buried there, including a daughter of Canute, Herbert of Bosham (the biographer of Thomas Becket) who died in 1186 and Earl Godwin, the father of King Harold. Tradition has it that Bosham was the site of Canute's demonstration to his flattering courtiers that he was unable to turn back the waves. The fact that an artificial embankment raised to keep back the sea was called a 'chair' in Sussex might demonstrate how the story might have become distorted. Despite its history, charms and curiosities, Bosham, although a great place to visit, especially on the quieter week days, is not exactly a first-choice day out by itself. With no beach, sand or facilities for bathing, it has been described as most suitable for "the tired and retired, the weekenders and the yachtsmen."

At the head of the same creek, Fishbourne is one of the largest and most significant Roman sites in England, not least because the archaeological record is illuminated in part by documentary evidence. Much closer to the sea in Roman times, archaeological evidence suggests that Fishbourne was the site of a major supply base and bridgehead, either at the time of, or shortly after, the main Roman invasion of Britain in AD 43. It was probably the main residence or palace of Tiberius Claudius Cogidubnus, a British client king and ally of the Romans, who is thought to have assisted the invasion and its subsequent penetration into the south-west. The extensive residence appears to have been the reward for him and his family for their cooperation.

The buildings at Fishbourne were built shortly afterwards, becoming over the next 30 years or so, one of the largest residential complexes in Roman Britain and comprising over 60 rooms grouped around a huge central courtyard. Clearly the centre of a large estate, the buildings were later in the 2nd and 3rd centuries re-designed and divided into separate residences. After the complex was destroyed by fire, possibly in a raid from the sea, in about 280, the site was

*Military Aviation Museum, **Tangmere***

Goodwood, built between 1780 and 1800

Flint built cottages in **Singleton**

The Spread Eagle Hotel, **Midhurst**

systematically cleared of all useful materials and the walls reduced to their foundations, probably with the stones used at Chichester nearby. The site was buried and forgotten until its re-discovery in 1960.

Much of the southern half of the site is covered by a road and modern buildings, but the extensive north wing, with over 20 mosaic floored rooms, has been fully excavated and protected by a purpose built structure that incorporates a museum. On show are numerous artefacts recovered from excavations, a hypocaust system and the mosaics for which Fishbourne is rightly famous, including one with a boy on a dolphin and another with cupids sparring as gladiators. The building offers opportunities for visitors to handle ancient artefacts and there is an imaginative education programme. Outside, the whole of the northern section of the Roman garden has been recreated, based on evidence from pollen, post-holes and other horticultural remains.

The Selsey Peninsula

Towards the coast in the south east of the rape, the place-names suggest that the low-lying land between Chichester and Selsey ('seal's island'), which nowhere rises above 30ft/9m, has been settled and cultivated at least since the early Saxon period. In Saxon times, Selsey really was an island, cut off from the mainland by the waters of Pagham harbour. All around, the coast-line between Pagham and Chichester harbours has been subject to continuous erosion, alteration and inundation ever since, to the extent that the original cathedral of Selsey, founded in the time of St Wilfrid, has completely disappeared into the sea, along with much of the original settlement. In Elizabethan times, the ruins of buildings could still be seen at low water and a great many Roman and other ancient artefacts were found on the beach in the 19th and early 20th centuries, including a hoard of a thousand 3rd century Roman coins. Selsey today, with its modern commercial development and dormitory settlement, is unremarkable, but there is a long stretch of sandy beach leading west to the Witterings and a Lifeboat Museum, with several de-commissioned lifeboats, as well as interesting photographs, a collection of memorabilia and an exhibition.

The coast to the north and west of Selsey is dominated by the popular, extensive shingle and sand beach-fronts of East and West Wittering and **Bracklesham Bay**. Bracklesham Bay is notable for the marine fossils and, occasionally, ancient items, that are found on the beach. **East Wittering** is a typical, bland sea-side residential settlement, but West Wittering, with its extensive beach and views out over the Solent at the eastern tip of Chichester Harbour has a far more pleasant atmosphere, although the town can become congested in summer (it was recently dubbed 'the Sussex Hamptons' (!) by Tatler magazine). Out of season, the walks along the coast to East Head are exhilarating. West Wittering also has the remains of a medieval manor of the bishops of Chichester, notably the early Tudor red-brick Cakeham Tower, which has long served as a sea mark. To the north-east of Selsey, **Pagham Harbour** was formed by a particularly intrusive inundation of the sea in 1910, resulting in a charming 1000ac/405ha salt-marsh Nature Reserve, which, despite being partially blighted by holiday and mobile homes, holds most national and international designations as a Site of Special Scientific Interest and is noted for its birdlife. There is an interpretation centre as **Sidlesham.** Pagham itself is an excellent base from which to explore the footpaths that lead around, with a pub en route, the edge of the harbour towards Church Norton, thought to be the site of St Wilfrid's monastery. In recent years, the area has become attractive to kite-surfers who use the sea at the harbour entrance.

Known as Bucgan ora (Bucgan's shore) in the 7th century, **Bognor** narrowly escaped being called Hothampton by a potential developer (Sir Richard Hotham) in the 18th century and gained its Regis post-nominal after George V recovered from illness there in 1928. It is at the centre of 7 miles of sandy beaches that stretch from Pagham to Middleton-on-Sea and has all the usual attractions, rides and amusements of a typical south coast sea-side resort. In addition, it has notably clean beaches and a promenade that is worth the effort of a walk.

There is a small, well-stocked museum of local history and colour on the High Street and **Hotham House**, built in 1792 by Sir Richard as his

---

Worth Visiting

The attractive village of **Apuldram** has a church, amid the fields, which has several interesting features, together with a manor house and Rymans, a medieval house, altered in the 17th century and later.

West Itchenor has been a sleepy amphibious village, but it has great views over Chichester Harbour and in the distance to the South Downs.

---

private residence, is probably one of the best Georgian houses in Sussex. Its 1000ft/305m pier, built in 1865, has seen better days and the seaward end is derelict and decaying fast, despite Grade II listing since 1989. It is the site of the annual (since 1978) **Bognor Birdman,** a competition for human powered flying machines held each summer, for which the prize is £30,000 for the furthest flight over 100 metres. Since 1998, Ron Freeman has won the event five years in succession, with his 2003 attempt reaching 270ft/82m).

To the east of Chichester, one of the most attractive parish churches in Sussex, **Boxgrove Priory** was originally a Benedictine house, founded in 1115, with the first phase of building continuing through to about 1220. The interior of the priory is a fine example of Norman (Romanesque) and Early English (Gothic) architecture and is unusual because it used to have both a secular nave and monastic choir, separated

*Remains of **Cowdray Castle***

Stansted Park

Bosham

by the crossing tower. The parochial nave, to the west, was demolished at the Dissolution, and the monastic choir was adopted as the new secular nave, which contains a magnificent chantry chapel, built in 1532 by Thomas West, 9th Lord de la Warr, lord of nearby Halnaker and patron of the priory. At the Dissolution, he tried to convince Thomas Cromwell to spare the priory, because in addition to his chapel, his ancestors and his wife's mother were buried there. In 1538, he had the ceiling painted with the arms and crests of his own and his wife's families, linked by flowers and foliage.

The guesthouse, now in ruins to the north of the priory, was where the Prior entertained guests and where travellers could find lodgings. In the 17th century, the churchwardens were repeatedly disciplined for playing cricket in the churchyard – "contrairie to the seventh article, and for that they used to breake windowes with the ball".

Nearby is the famous Battle of Britain Airfield of Tangmere, of which little recognisable remains amid extensive nurseries and other modern development. On site is a particularly enjoyable Military Aviation Museum, which has a comprehensive collection of aircraft types housed in a number of exhibition halls, as well as a good insight into life at Tangmere during its active service. There are also three flight simulators, including the cockpit of a Hawker Hunter Mk 4 jet aircraft that test the skills of both young and old.

Further east, Fontwell Park Racecourse is set in beautiful countryside, just by the roundabout joining the A27 and A29, and its figure of eight course has been voted the best small racecourse in the south-east. As well as race meetings, there are frequent events including car rallies and exhibitions. Also at Fontwell is the innovative 4ac/1.6ha **Denman's Gardens**, designed by Michael Neve and John Brookes to give inspiration to owners of small gardens. Alongside an award winning café, a wide variety of shrubs and perennials are for sale.

Just north and east of Chichester and at the foot of the Downs is the beautiful park and country house of **Goodwood**, the seat of those Stuarts descended from Charles II and his mistress, Louise de Querouaille, built by James Wyatt in Sussex flint 1780-1800 to enclose a brick predecessor (1720) for the third Duke of Richmond. The original design was to be a huge octagon with towers at each corner, but this proved to be too expensive and only three sides were completed. Its spacious, light, mirrored rooms contain a rich collection of period furniture, porcelain and paintings, including numerous pictures of various members of the Stuart dynasty, all the way back to Charles I, notably by Van Dyck and Lely. Other masterpieces include works by Stubbs, Hogarth, Kneller and Canaletto and superb Gobelin tapestries. It is hard to believe that during the Second World War the house was used as a hospital. High above the house on the Downs, **Goodwood racecourse** was built 1801-2 and the summer race

meetings are an unusual treat. Known familiarly as 'Glorious Goodwood', they are, with their easy accessibility and unforced informality, a wonderful way to spend long summer days out at the races. Next to the racecourse is the **Trundle**, a prehistoric settlement that was active for about 2000 years before the Romans arrived and whose three concentric rings of earthwork fortifications, built as the tribal centre of the Regni from the 5th century BC onwards, stand out against the skyline. Also nearby, on the site of the Battle of Britain airfield of Westhampnett, is a motor racing circuit that saw racing 1948-66, but which was closed to competitive activity because of the potential danger to spectators from increasingly powerful vehicles. It is still used as a leisure airfield and for testing, rallies and various events, such as the annual Goodwood Festival of Speed and the Goodwood Revival.

Worth Visiting

The **Cass Sculpture Foundation** is sited in 26 acres of ancient woodland on the Sussex Downs. Over 80 large works are on display in evocative surroundings and for sale, so that new works can be commissioned. The Foundation, which has a library, archive and visualisation centre has commissioned 160 monumental works from over 120 artists – all of which have been sold, with the profits divided between the artist and the Foundation.

Moving up the Lavant valley, **Singleton** has a pretty cluster of flint built cottages and a fine church that has a Saxon tower and nave, as well as a host of early and late medieval features, mostly from the 15th century. The thoroughly worthwhile and absorbing **Weald and Downland Museum** at Singleton was founded in 1966 as a home for historical domestic and working buildings that could not be preserved or might face destruction in their original locations. The 45 or so buildings on the 50ac/20ha site, all from the south-east of England, date from the 13th to the 19th century. All were carefully dismantled and re-erected in their current setting amid period gardens, farm animals and woodland walks. There is also a working water mill and lively demonstrations of traditional Downland industries and crafts.

West Dean is a 6,400ac/2590ha estate on the western South Downs whose gardens have probably the finest Victorian glasshouses in the country, along with a restored, walled kitchen garden and an inspiring circular walk through a 49ac/20ha arboretum. There is a 300ft/91m Edwardian pergola, ornamental beds and a pond, along with a good restaurant and gift and produce shop. The house itself, built in 1804, but almost totally re-modelled in the 1890s is one of the finest flint-faced buildings in England and is the centre for the Edward James Foundation, a college which promotes the study of conservation, arts and crafts, writing, gardening and music.

A Roman crossing point over the river Rother and a medieval market,

Midhurst stands between the heath and woodland of the greensand hills to its north and one of the most attractive, wooded sections of the Downs to the south. As such, it is a good centre for walking and exploring some of the lesser known and unhurried parts of West Sussex. It has two well-known and ancient inns – the Angel and the Spread-Eagle, a 15th century building – and a curfew bell that tolls every night at eight o'clock. The old streets and their buildings of various timber-framed and brick construction are well worth a look, especially in Lion Street (with its 16th century houses left stranded on an island by 18th century road widening), South Street, with its Market Hall (1552) and Knockhundred Row.

Just to the east of the market square is a small mound overlooking the Rother that is occupied by the foundations of the fortified manor house of the de Bohuns, the original lords of Midhurst, which was abandoned in 1280 in favour of the site at Cowdray. North Street gives access across the river Rother to the ruins of this imposing early Tudor mansion that was begun in 1492 and completed between 1529 and 1542, most notably by Sir Anthony Browne. After he had used the lands and proceeds that he had acquired after the dissolution of Battle Abbey and other church properties in 1538 to fund the building, the family was said to be have been cursed by a monk of Battle that they would perish by fire and water. Although they soon became Viscounts Montagu and very rich, Cowdray was destroyed by fire in 1793; a week later, the last

37

Viscount Montagu drowned while attempting to pass through the Falls of Laufenberg on the river Rhine and, in the same year, his two nephews were drowned at Bognor. Today, the ruins are remarkable for their extent and multitude of preserved early 16th architectural details. The Polo Gold Cup Final takes place here on the estate every year.

Worth Visiting

A restored Tudor garden opened at Cowdray in 2005 and continues to develop. It currently includes Tudor geometric beds, together with herb garden, perennial borders, rose-walkways and fruit trees. **Iping common** and **Stedham Commons** are a local nature reserve and the Special Scientific Interest habitat for various species that thrive on lowland heath.

Between Midhurst and Petersfield, **Trotton** has a handsome early 15th century bridge, but is most remarkable for the contents of its interesting medieval church (St George), the nave and chancel of which date from about 1300 and its roof from about 1400. With a tower of about 1230 that seems to have survived from an earlier church, it has 14th century frescoes depicting, among other themes, Christ in Judgement, Moses and the Tablets of the Law and the Seven Deadly Sins. Set into the nave floor is a brass of Margaret de Camoys (who died about 1310), the oldest of a female in England, with a Norman-French inscription. In the chancel is the ornately canopied table-tomb and impressive brass of another Lady Camoys, alongside her second husband Thomas who died in 1421. She was Elizabeth Mortimer whose first husband had been Harry 'Hotspur', the son of the earl of Northumberland who was killed fighting Henry IV at the battle of Shrewsbury in 1403. The Lewknor family tombs are of interest, as is the inscription to Thomas Otway, the 17th century poet and playwright.

Moving west, on the western fringes of the rape, **South Harting** is one of the best villages in West Sussex to visit for a day trip, mostly because of the access it gives to the sweeping countryside of the Hampshire/Sussex border, but also because of the busy charm of the place itself. As well as the hospitable Ship Inn (17th century and made of ship's timbers), cottages made of timber and lathe and plaster are all around, 18th century houses give the village its air of solid respectability and, just to make sure, a whipping post and stocks still stand by the church. The church is mainly 14th century, with a 130ft/40m tower and (rebuilt) spire, although there are substantial traces of Saxon and early medieval work throughout the nave and its arcades. There are memorials to the Fords and Featherstonhaughs of nearby Uppark.

The South Downs Way, taking in the dramatic northern scarp of the Downs, passes close by to the south of the village, but some of the best walks in the area are along foot and bridle paths that take in the villages known as **The Mardens**, each of which has a beautifully distinctive church of unmodified Saxon or Norman origin to visit. The routes to **Beacon Hill** and **Treyford Hill** are also particularly enjoyable, as are those to **Compton**, **Up Marden** and **Chilgrove**. Probably the best route is that which leads south from Chilgrove (with a good pub) to Bow Hill and on to **West Stoke**, which takes in spectacular views and **Kingley Vale** famous for its yews that are supposed to have been planted over the grave pits of Danes killed in a battle in 895. Just south of South Harting is Uppark. On the site of a former 15th century house owned by the Ford family and with commanding views from the top of the Downs, **Uppark** was built for the first Lord Tankerville in about 1690. However, the house was significantly re-modelled by Sir Matthew and Lady Sarah Fetherstonhaugh 1750 – 1760 and stocked with many items that they had collected on their Grand Tour in 1749-1751. Their son, Sir Harry Fetherstonhaugh, added to the collection and a pillared portico, dairy and landscaped garden, as well as a mistress, the young Emma Hart (later Lady Hamilton). At the age of over seventy, Sir Harry married his dairy maid to whom he left the house. In 1954, the house was given to the National Trust.

In 1989, Uppark suffered a devastating fire caused by a worker's blowtorch. Works of art and furniture were removed from the burning building by members of the Meade-Fetherstonhaugh family, National Trust staff and the visiting public. Afterwards, only the walls were left standing, but, happily, most of the contents had been saved and the house re-opened after a full restoration in 1995. The author, H G Wells spent part of his boyhood at Uppark, where his mother was housekeeper 1880-1893. The house features as 'Bladesover' in his semi-autobiographical work 'Tono-Bungay'. To the south, **Stansted Park** is an Edwardian country house at the heart of a 1,750ac/705ha estate, with extensive woodlands and agricultural land. It is the fictional country house that appears in P G Wodehouse's Lord Emsworth stories. Wodehouse lived at nearby Emsworth and many of his characters are named after local places.

The site of **Stansted** was occupied by a hunting lodge in the Forest of Bere in the 11th century and, although the house built in 1688 at the same time as Uppark was destroyed by fire in 1900, the present building, constructed in 1903, is a faithful replica of its predecessor. Purchased by the Bessborough family in 1924 and owned by the 9th and 10th Earls throughout their lifetimes, the House and Estate have been owned since 1983 by a charitable trust. Today, it has a fine Garden Centre, the Pavilion Tea Room in the walled garden and a Light Railway. The surrounding estate has several good walking routes, one of which was (really) used by Charles II during his escape from the battle of Worcester in 1651.

Places to Visit

Bognor Regis Museum
69 High St PO21 1RY
☎ 01243 865636
www.bognor-regis.org/bognor
/br_museum.html
Open: Apr-Oct, Tues-Sun, 10am-4pm
and BH Mon

Boxgrove Priory
Church Lane Boxgrove PO18 OED
☎ 01243 774045
English Heritage.
Open any reasonable time in daylight
hours
www.boxgrovepriory.co.uk

Chichester:

Chichester Cathedral
West Street Chichester PO19 1PX
☎ 01243 782595
www.chichestercathedral.org.uk
Open: 7.15am-6pm in winter and until
7pm in summer

Chichester District Museum
29 Little London Chichester PO19 1PB
☎ 01243 784683
www.chichester.gov.uk/museum
Open: all year Wed-Sat 10am-5.30pm

Chichester Festival Theatre
Oaklands Park Chichester PO19 6AP
☎ 01243 781312
www.cft.org.uk" www.cft.org.uk
See website for theatre programme

Pallant House Gallery
9 North Pallant Chichester PO19 1TJ
☎ 01243 774557
www.pallant.org.uk
Open: Tues-Sat, 10am-5pm (8pm on
Thurs), Sun & BH 12.30-5pm

South Downs Planetarium & Science Centre
Sir Patrick Moore Building Kingsham
Farm Kingsham Road PO19 8RP
☎ 01243 774400
www.southdowns.org.uk
For monthly show times see website

Cowdray House Ruins & Park
Midhurst GU29 9AL
☎ 01730 810781
www.cowdray.org.uk
Open: mid-Mar to Oct, Wed-Sun
10.30am-5pm

Cowdray Tudor Walled Garden
No.1 River Ground Stables Cowdray
Park GU29 9AL
☎ 01730 816881 1 River Ground
Stables
www.walledgardencowdray.co.uk
Open: Wed-Sun, 10am-5pm

Fishbourne Roman Palace
Salthill Road Fishbourne Chichester
PO19 3QR
☎ 01243 785859
www.sussexpast.co.uk/fishbourne
Open: daily Feb-Nov, 10am -4pm (5pm
Mar-Oct), limited opening Jan & Dec

Goodwood House
Goodwood Chichester PO18 0PX
☎ 01243 755040
www.goodwood.co.uk
Open: late May to mid-Oct, Sun & Mon,
Aug Sun-Thurs, 1-5pm
The house is closed during Festival of
Speed and Goodwood Revival. Check
website or call.

Selsey Lifeboat Station
The Boathouse Kingsway PO20 0DL
☎ 01243 601866
www.selseylifeboats.co.uk
Please call to check opening times

Stansted Park

Rowlands Castle PO9 6DX

☎ 023 9241 2265

www.stanstedpark.co.uk

Open: Easter-Sept, Sun-Wed, 1-4pm

Tangmere Military Aviation Museum

Tangmere Nr Chichester PO20 2ES

☎ 01243 790090

www.tangmere-museum.org.uk

Open: every day Feb-Nov, 10am-4.30pm (5.30pm Mar-Oct)

Uppark

South Harting Near Petersfield GU31 5QR

☎ 01730 825857

www.nationaltrust.org.uk/main /w-uppark

House open Apr-Oct Sun-Thurs, 12.30-5pm (Gardens open at 11.30am)

Weald and Downland Open Air Museum

Singleton PO18 0EU

☎ 01243 811363

www.wealddown.co.uk

Open: daily Mar-23 Dec; Boxing Day and New Year's Day for special seasonal event; Jan-Feb, Sat & Sun; Open: 10.30am-6pm British Summer Time; 10.30am-4pm all other times

Gardens

Cass Sculpture Foundation Goodwood PO18 0QP

☎ 01243 538449

Open: late March to end Oct, Tues-Sun 10:30am-5:00pm (last entry at 4:00pm

Denman's Garden

Denman's Lane, Fontwell BN18 0SU

☎ 01243 542808

www.denmansgarden.co.uk

Open: daily all year. Closed 25, 26 Dec & 1 Jan

Earnley Butterflies & Gardens

133 Almodington Lane Earnley Chichester PO20 7JR

☎ 01243 512637

www.earnleybutterfliesandgardens. co.uk

Open: Easter-Oct, 10am-6pm

West Dean Gardens

West Dean PO18 OQZ

☎ 01243 811301

www.westdean.org.uk

Open: all year 10.30am-4pm (5pm Mar-Oct), closed Christmas and all January

Racecourses

Fontwell Park Racecourse

Arundel Road Fontwell BN18 0SX

☎ 01243 543335

www.fontwellpark.co.uk

For events and racing fixtures see website

Goodwood Racecourse

Goodwood PO18 0PS

www.goodwood.co.uk"

www.goodwood.co.uk

Racing from May-Oct

Glorious Goodwood – end of July

2. THE RAPE OF ARUNDEL

Arundel and its imposing castle dominate the gap in the Downs formed by the River Arun. It is a prosperous and confident market town which was a port of some importance in the medieval and early modern periods, notably for the export of timber and other trade along its navigable river. It has a variety of historic buildings within a small area, reflecting the character and footprint of its medieval origins, although most timber-framed buildings are covered by later facades. Two late medieval buildings survive in the High Street, 37–41 and No. 71 is a Wealden house. Most of the public and commercial buildings are 19th century, with nods to various historical periods, in brick, flint or sandstone.

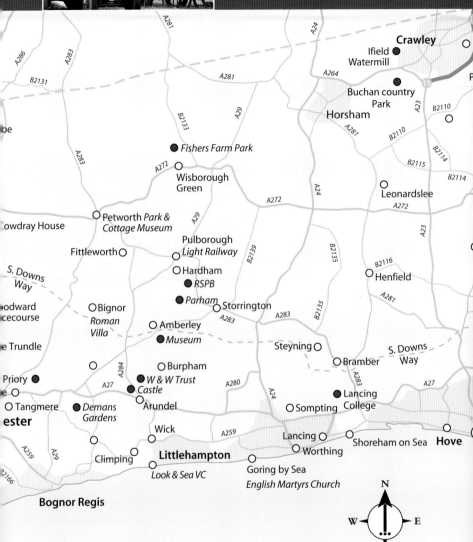

Crawley

Ifield ●
Watermill

Buchan country
Park ●

Horsham

● Fishers Farm Park

Wisborough
Green

○ Leonardslee

Petworth ○ *Park &*
Cottage Museum

Fittleworth ○

Pulborough
Light Railway

○ Hardham

Henfield ○

● RSPB

● *Parham*

Storrington ○

○ Bignor
Roman
Villa

○ Amberley
● *Museum*

Steyning ○

S. Downs
Way

○ Burpham

○ Bramber

Lancing ●
College

● W & W Trust
○ *Castle*

○ Sompting

○ Arundel

● *Demans*
Gardens

○ Tangmere

Wick ○

Lancing ○

Hove

Shoreham on Sea

○ Worthing

Climping ○

Littlehampton

Look & Sea VC

Goring by Sea
English Martyrs Church

Bognor Regis

Cowdray House

S. Downs
Way

Priory ●

Trundle

ester

N
W — E
S

The honour and rape of Arundel were granted to the turbulent, possibly unstable, Roger de Montgomery after the battle of Hastings and he immediately constructed a motte-and-bailey **castle**. The medieval castle was subsequently acquired and progressively strengthened by the Fitzalan and Howard families, the latter becoming Dukes of Norfolk at the end of the 15th century. The Howards were notable dynasts and leading political figures throughout the Tudor period. After the Civil War, in 1645, the castle was slighted, or partially demolished, but was restored to its present condition by Henry, the 15th Duke of Norfolk who succeeded in 1860 and died in 1917. As a result, one sees today a mix of medieval fortress, with the 11th century Norman keep and 13th century gatehouse and barbican and a romantically conceived Victorian country house (what has been called 'an unfeeling Windsor Castle style'). Nevertheless, the familiar Gothic splendour, with its breathtaking library converted from a Tudor gallery, the Barons' Hall, the chapel and the dining room, along with portraits, furniture and a profusion of family acquisitions – including the sword taken from the dead James IV of Scotland at the battle of Flodden in 1513 make for a memorable visit. The estate grounds are fun to explore and include the **Swanbourne Lake** plus the cricket ground on which all touring test sides play against a select Duke or Duchess of Norfolk XI and The Collector Earl's Garden.

A rewarding walk to **Burpham** just to the east of Arundel takes in the river and crosses the railway. The village is the site of the substantial Saxon fortified burgh that preceded Arundel and the earthworks can still be seen, along with a handsome 12-13th century church, with distinctive Norman features. For the energetic, the walk can continue to Amberley and beyond.

North of Arundel

Set back from the Downs amid water meadows and overlooking the Wild Brooks (probably a former medieval fishpond or lake), **Amberley** is one of the most attractive villages in West Sussex, based on what has been called its "enchanting irregularity". It has carefully tended gardens and neat, picturesque houses and thatched cottages, as well as a fine church and castle at its west end. The tea-rooms in the village offer a welcome respite. Probably begun in the late 11th century, this interesting church retains much characteristic Norman work, together with the remains of later medieval wall paintings and a 13th century chancel and south aisle. The tower and the south doorway are 14th century.

Amberley Castle was built in the last two decades of the 14th century as a fortified manor of the bishops of Chichester, probably on the site of, and incorporating, a Norman and early medieval predecessor. It is a rough quadrangular courtyard structure which is approached through

Worth Visiting

The parish church of St Nicholas was built in 1381 on the site of a Benedictine Priory in the Perpendicular style. It is both Anglican and Roman Catholic, with a glass screen dividing off the chancel from the nave and transepts (reflecting a 19th century dispute between the vicar and a Roman Catholic Duke and a subsequent brick wall).

The Roman Catholic Cathedral of St Philip Howard was designed by Joseph Hansom (of the cab fame) and built 1868-73, in the French Gothic style. Plans for a tower over the entrance were abandoned because the foundations were inadequate.

Arundel Museum and Heritage Centre – a Grade II listed building that brings to life the varied history of Arundel and its surrounding area.

The Wildfowl & Wetlands Trust in Mill Road gives visitors the chance to see hundreds of the ducks, wildfowl and swans from around the world at close quarters in delightful surroundings in the lee of the castle. It has 26 hectares of naturalised landscapes and wetland habitats and free safaris are available on electric boats. The visitor centre has a good restaurant.

Worth a glance: The ruins of the Maison Dieu (near the bridge), a hospice for 'twenty poor men, aged or infirm, but of good life' was established in 1395, but dissolved and dismantled in 1540. Its stones went to make the bridge.

a twin-towered gate-house over a dry moat that used to be wet. Inside, there is a 16th century bishop's residence, most of which is today occupied by a luxury hotel, with 19 distinctively decorated rooms.

Nearby, **Amberley Museum** and Heritage Centre is situated around old chalk workings on a 36 acre attraction. Its wide range of exhibits and collections recreates and preserves the industrial heritage of the south-east of England and there is a lot for children and adults to see and do. The site is fully accessible by free rides on a vintage bus or miniature railway service and comprises exhibitions of working tradecraft and hands-on experiences, as well as many aspects of industrial development, including energy and electricity, roads and road-making and other historic processes. There are also several nature trails and opportunities to walk amid the former workings, as well as frequent themed special events throughout the year.

Walk

Start in Amberley village and walk towards the B2139. Take care crossing this busy road and begin a short, sharp climb up Mill Lane until you reach a

Arundel castle

Arundel Cathedral

Arundel Farmers' market

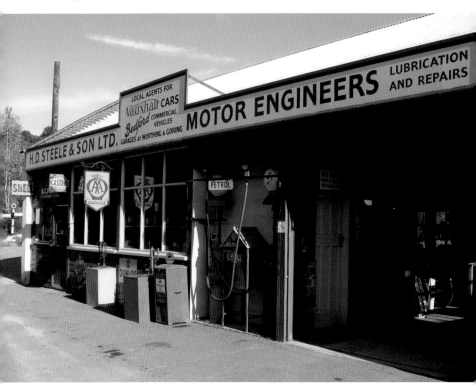

Amberley Working Museum

house called High Down on the left. Shortly afterwards, turn left onto the South Downs Way and climb up Amberley Mount. As you ascend, outstanding views open in all directions. To the left, on a clear day you can see all the way across the valley of the meandering Arun and its flood plain to the North Downs and beyond, while to the right, across downland and wheat fields, there is a distant prospect of Littlehampton and the sea. As you make your way along the ridge, Arundel Castle can be clearly seen, dominating the Arun valley to the south, with the Isle of Wight and (on a sunny day) Portsmouth's Spinnaker Tower. There are plenty of prehistoric remains along the way, as well as (at the right time of the year) a host of wild flowers (birdsfoot trefoil, cornflowers, wild thyme and campion) and various butterflies.

Continue along the ridge, past Springhead Hill and its car park, to Chantry Post, where you take the bridleway south that is signposted to Lee Farm, with the prehistoric settlement and flint mines on Harrow Hill ahead of you. Turning right, go through the busy working farm on a metalled and gravel track and, on arrival at Wepham Down, be sure to take a path heading north until you reach a field boundary with a bridleway heading west. Take this route until you come to an intersection of paths. Turn

left and then immediately right, heading for a small triangular wood, and on entering the wood, take the first footpath on the right. This gentle incline crosses another path at right angles. Continue straight ahead and descend into a steep cleft in the downs before turning right to pass through a gate in a fence. Immediately turn left and climb through a small wood to emerge on a gentle slope leading back up to the ridge. Join the ridge just to the west of Amberley Mount and return to Amberley village the way you came.

Further west, where it is extremely well-positioned on fertile, south-facing greensand, Stane Street, the main Roman road from London to Chichester, passes close to **Bignor Roman villa.** Built early in the 2nd century, but progressively abandoned after AD 300, possibly in response to Saxon raids, the villa in its heyday probably controlled the activities and output of an estate of 4000 acres of arable and grazing land. Covering almost 5 acres, the villa itself comprised about 65 rooms that surrounded a courtyard, along with several outlying farm buildings, storehouses and granaries. Most of the later additions were made in the north wing, where most of the site's excellent mosaics are displayed, including the nationally significant Ganymede, Medusa and Venus and Cupid representations. The site also has a first-rate museum and interpretation facility, as well as the obligatory hypocaust.

Bignor village has 3 notable buildings, which are each worth a look in passing. The Church of the Holy Cross is a mostly 13th century structure, but is of Saxon origin as evidenced by the 11th century chancel arch and font surviving from the 11th century. The 15th century oak-framed hall house known as the Yeoman's House is a Wealden type, with a recessed centre section with curved brackets supporting the eaves, while the first floor of the wings projects beyond the walls of plaster and flint filling. The Manor House was used as a secret forward base for preparing, training and debriefing agents working with the French resistance and members of the Special Operations Executive (SOE) during World War II.

Slindon, south-west of Bignor, is a 3,507ac/420ha estate of farm and woodland that includes Bignor and Coldharbour Hills, Glatting Beacon, a good stretch of the South Downs Way and most of Slindon village, with its 17th-century flint cottages. The estate was acquired by the National Trust between 1950 and 1970 and offers numerous opportunities for good walking and long views.

North-east of Arundel

To the north-east, **Parham**, near Storrington, used to be a grange of the monks of Westminster until the Dissolution and traces of the medieval work can be seen in the north-east wing. In 1577-80, the Palmer family built the Elizabethan mansion, complete with the 160 feet Long Gallery. In 1601, it was bought by Thomas Bysshop and the estate was later developed further by removing the small village of Parham and modernising the small 16th century church. Today, after careful restoration from the 1920s onwards, Parham is acknowledged as being one of the most striking late Tudor mansions in the county. It has a particularly fine collection of historic furniture, paintings and textiles, as well as 16th century needlework and carpets, which, unusually, are complemented by a large number of 20th century items. The portraits, by Lely, Gainsborough and Romney among others are superb in their settings, especially those of the Stuarts and the families that have been associated with Parham over the centuries.

Outside, the four-acre walled garden has large mixed borders and greenhouses, which are mostly dedicated to providing flowers and plants for the house. Landscaped grounds dating from the 18th century cover seven acres and include an ornamental lake, numerous trees and shrubs and a brick and turf maze. The house and gardens are enclosed by an estate of 875ac/354ha of working farm and woodland, which includes 300ac/121ha of ancient park and roe and fallow deer, descendants of a 1628 herd. The Monument is a prospect tower that offers good views over the park and towards the Downs in the distance.

Slindon

Parham Steam Rally

Petworth House

Parham House, Storrington

51

To the north, Stane Street crossed the Arun where Pulborough now stands and Roman remains have been found in the area. During Saxon and medieval times, it was an important overnight and watering stop for drovers. It has an imposingly large 13th century church, with tower, nave and transepts effectively rebuilt in the early 15th century in the Perpendicular style and a distinctive lych-gate. The Chequers Hotel is a 15th century house which has the remains of a medieval priory chapel in its garden. In a most attractive setting, Stopham Bridge was built 1309 and re-built in 1403 and six of its original arches remain – the seventh was added in 1822. The town holds annual lawn mower and duck (August Bank Holiday) races. The excellent **South Downs Light Railway** (10$\frac{1}{4}$ in (260 mm) gauge), with its steam and diesel trains, runs regularly throughout the summer, with a reduced service at other times. To the south-east, the **RSPB's Pulborough Brooks** nature reserve in the Arun Valley has a wealth of wildlife and birds, as well as a nature trails and visitor centre that hosts a tearoom, shop and play area.

Nearby at **Hardham**, the delightful church of St Botolph's dates from about 1100 and contains some remarkable wall paintings, all of famous biblical scenes, thought to have been executed by the monks at Lewes Priory. Nearby are the earthwork remains, cut through by the railway, of a Roman posting station (like today's motorway services) that stood on Stane Street, much of whose building material is contained in the fabric of the church.

Between Pulborough and Petworth, the Swan Inn at the picturesque village of **Fittleworth** is famous as the home of the Ancient Order of Froth Blowers, founded in 1924 'to foster the noble Art and gentle and healthy Pastime of froth blowing amongst Gentlemen of-leisure and ex-Soldiers'. Extraordinarily popular in the 1920s and 1930s, lager was forbidden, as 'it is unseemly and should be avoided always excepting by Naval Officers visiting German Colonies'. The local area was a haunt of Sir Edward Elgar and Sir Hubert Parry.

To the north, with origins that are recorded at least back to the 8th century, the attractive town of **Petworth** retains much of its old world charm, with its timber-framed shops and brick Georgian houses. As well as the town hall and market square, the heavily restored early medieval, but predominantly 14th century parish church is worth a look on account of several interesting features and monuments, as are the Somerset Hospital and Lodge and the Tudor House (although built in 1629), opposite the church. William Cobbett, the social reformer, lived in the town. **Petworth Cottage Museum** is a period house that has been restored and furnished in the style of the year 1910, with various artefacts and furnishings relating to the period and the seamstress who lived there 1901-1930.

The town is dominated by the palatial **Petworth House**, the traditional family seat of, successively, the Percy, Seymour and Wyndham families and which is possibly the most compellingly interesting country house in Sussex. A fortified manor house was erected on the site in 1293 by Henry, Lord Percy, a powerful northern magnate, whose descendants became the earls (and dukes) of Northumberland and, while progressively improving Petworth, acquired a profusion of other distinguished titles down to the 20th century.

Administered since 1947 by the National Trust and standing in its own extensive park, the present house was built 1688-96 by Charles Seymour, 6th Duke of Somerset, of local stone, with Portland stone dressings, and largely retains its original appearance, including its immediately striking 320ft long west front. The building incorporated and improved the original medieval chapel, but its major attraction is its interconnected series of magnificent rooms that contain a seemingly endless profusion of furniture, sculptures, porcelain and pictures, including a nationally and internationally significant collection of paintings that began with works mostly by Van Dyck, Lely and several 17th century English and Dutch masters. The most prolific owner and patron was George O'Brien Wyndham, the third earl of Egremont, who between 1795 and 1835, added 263 works by 66 notable artists (they read like a history of art) to the existing collection and sponsored and commissioned Romney and Turner to paint a large number of family and local scenes. The wood carvings by Grinling Gibbons are exceptionally fine.

Right at the top of the rape is the highest point in Sussex (280 metres /919 feet). With its pine and heather covered slopes, **Blackdown Hill** is very popular with walkers. Between 1796 and 1816, it had a shutter telegraph station that passed signals between the Admiralty in London and the Fleet in Portsmouth. The view from the summit is quite remarkable in all directions, across the Weald, into Hampshire and as far as Mount Harry near Lewes (30 miles away).

On its eastern slope is **Aldworth**, originally bought as a 60ac/24ha estate in 1867, by Alfred, Lord Tennyson. He built the house as a summer residence, with running hot water, away from the crowds that used to beset him at Farringford in the Isle of Wight. Designed by Sir James Knowles and later rather unkindly and airily labelled by Nikolaus Pevsner as "a fussy small hotel", Tennyson waxed lyrically about its magnificent views down to the sea. He died in the house on 6 October 1892. Near Wisborough Green, **Fishers Farm Park** is a combination of rural farmyard, with animal contact opportunities and an indoor and outdoor adventure play area, probably best suited for families, in particular the under-11s.

On the Coast

Down on the coast, **Littlehampton** flourished as a port in the Middle Ages by importing produce and Caen stone – to build churches and castles in Sussex – from Normandy. Subsequently, alongside fishing, it attracted various worthies in the late 18th century, including Byron, Coleridge, Shelley and Constable and it remained a busy port into the 19th century. It has a busy harbour area and marina with lots of restaurants and cafés, and gives access via a ferry to the west to **Climping Sands**. This huge beach has dunes and good walks, as well as 2½ miles/4km of coastline for sandy bathing, amid the rocks, and 1000ac/404ha of National Trust land, popular with bird-watchers and naturalists. The town's noteworthy attraction is **Harbour Park**, which has a wide variety of rides, flumes and family amusements, such as Fantasy Golf, the Horror Hotel and the Log Flume, as well as an indoor rink.

Further west, the church at **Yapton** is worth a detour. It dates from the 12th and 13th centuries and has not suffered Victorian modernisation, with external walls that are only 5ft/1.5m high, supporting a steep tie-beam roof. The question – 'Were you born in Yapton?' – in response to someone who has forgotten to shut a door is believed to refer to the 18th century tendency to leave doors open or unlocked so that smugglers could hide their goods in the nearest house when they were pursued by Excise men.

To the east, **Rustington** is a seaside resort, although access to the beach except on foot is difficult. It contains a conservation area with many Grade II Listed buildings, notably some fine 17th and 18th century Sussex flint cottages. Sir Hubert Parry wrote the music for Blake's Jerusalem here. At **Goring-by-**

Worth Visiting

Look and Sea Heritage Exhibition Centre is a new venture whose viewing tower gives one of the best all-round views in Sussex. The Exhibition deals with the seaside and the maritime history of Littlehampton. **The East Beach Cafe**, on the seafront, is a welded monocoque structure, which is supposed to resemble 'a piece of weathered flotsam swept up onto the beach'.

To the west of Littlehampton are two delightful churches that both date and contain notable features from Norman times. **Climping** has a very solid 45 ft high tower, built for defensive purposes, along with an elegant west door and later medieval fittings. **Ford** combines a simple Saxon nave of about 1050 with a Norman chancel, together with 15th century wall paintings.

Sea, the church of the English Martyrs has a remarkable interior, decorated with a two-third scale replica of the ceiling of the Sistine Chapel, painted by Gary Bevans 1988-93.

Nutbourne Vineyard and Windmill, Pulborough

Places to Visit

Amberley Museum and Heritage Centre
Near Arundel BN18 9LT
☎ 01798 831370
www.amberleymuseum.co.uk"
www.amberleymuseum.co.uk
Open: mid-Feb to Oct

Arundel Castle
BN18 9AB
☎ 01903 882173
www.arundelcastle.org
Open: Tues-Sun (Mondays in August)
and BH Mons, 10am-5pm. Castle
Rooms open 12-5pm

RC Arundel Cathedral of St Philip Howard
Parson's Hill Arundel BN18 9AY
☎ 01903 882297
www.arundelcathedral.org
Open: daily 9am-5pm

Arundel Museum
Located in the History Store Car Park
Mill Road *
☎ 01903 882456
www.arundelmuseum.org.uk
Open: 11am-3pm
*Temporary location at time of writing

Bignor Roman Villa
Bignor Lane Bignor RH20 1PH
www.bignorromanvilla.co.uk
☎ 01798 869259
Open: daily Mar-Oct, 10am-5pm (6pm
in June, July & Aug)

English Martyrs Catholic Church
Goring Way Goring by Sea
BN12 4UH
☎ 01903 506890
www.sistinechapeluk.co.uk
Open daily

Littlehampton Harbour Park
Seafront Littlehampton BN17 5LL
☎ 01903 721200
www.harbourpark.com
For opening times check website

Look and Sea Visitor Centre
63-65 Surrey Street Littlehampton
BN17 5AW
☎ 01903 718984
www.lookandsea.co.uk
Open: daily from 9am

Parham House
Storrington Nr Pulborough RH20 4HS
☎ 01903 742021
www.parhaminsussex.co.uk
Open: Easter Sunday-Sept, Wed,
Thurs, Sun & BH Mons 2-5pm.
Also open Tues & Fri in August

Petworth House
Petworth GU28 0AE
☎ 01798 343929
www.nationaltrust.org.uk
Open: mid-March to Oct, Sat to Wed,
11am-5pm
Open: Good Friday

Petworth Cottage Museum

346 High St Petworth GU28 0AU

☎ 01798 342100

www.petworthcottagemuseum.co.uk

Open: Apr-Oct, Tues-Sat 2-4.30pm & Bank Holidays

South Downs Light Railway

Pulborough Garden Centre Stopham Road Pulborough RH20 1DS

☎ 01798 872981

www.sdlr.com

For opening times see website

Country Parks, Farm Parks & Nature Reserves

Arundel Wildfowl Trust

Mill Road Arundel BN18 9PB

☎ 01903 883355

www.wwt.org.uk

Open: daily except 25 Dec, 9.30am-4.30pm (5.30pm in summer)

Fishers Farm Park

Newpound Lane Wisborough Green RH14 0EG

☎ 01403 700063

www.fishersfarmpark.co.uk

Open: daily 10am-5pm except 25 & 26 Dec

RSPB Pulborough Brooks

Off A283 2 miles south of Pulborough

☎ 01798 875851

Visitor centre open daily 9am-5.30pm. Free for RSPB members.

3. THE RAPE OF BRAMBER

Worthing Pier

Much of the hinterland of the rape of Bramber reflects the north-south orientation and pattern of its neighbours, with the settlement – and in the past, political power - concentrated in the south on a river valley on the coastal plain. Moving north, one passes across the sparsely occupied uplands of the chalk Downs, before descending firstly to the greensand levels and finally to the clay, marsh and sand of The Weald. Beyond the Downs, the villages reflect the pattern of clearance and settlement, with small communities and churches that have their origins in the Saxon and Norman periods. In the north of the rape of Bramber, east of Horsham is St Leonard's Forest, one of the last substantial swathes of forest. The north of the rape also has the greatest concentration of residential and commercial development, both current and planned, based on Horsham, Crawley and Gatwick Airport.

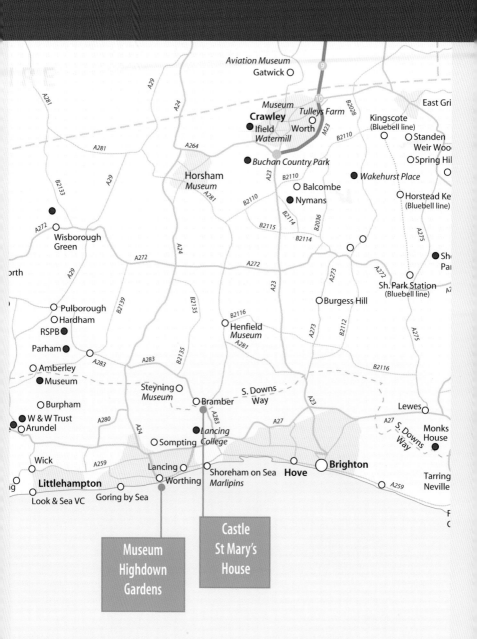

The castle at **Bramber** was built by William de Braose in the 1070s to dominate the gap in the Downs made by the valley of the river Adur, to guard the port of Steyning and to serve as the administrative centre of the rape. Now owned by the National Trust, it was of classic motte-and-bailey construction and later strongly re-built in stone. Held successively by the powerful and historically significant de Braose, Mowbray and Howard families, it was captured and mostly demolished by Parliamentary forces in the Civil War (1642-5). Fragments of stonework remain today, but the site is well worth a visit and is an excellent place for children to let off steam.

The nearby church of **St Nicholas** was built as a chapel for the castle in Norman times and retains some original features, despite being knocked about when used as a gun emplacement by Parliamentary troops in the Civil War. It also suffered when the castle was dismantled and a massive section of the keep fell on the chancel. Subsequent restorations have not helped.

Bramber village, based around a main street that stretches from the castle to the river Adur, is extremely attractive and includes the delightful **St Mary's**, a former medieval pilgrims' hospice that houses an interesting collection of curios, imaginative gardens and a welcome tea-room.

From the 8th century, **Steyning** was a place of pilgrimage to the shrine of St Cuthman and, as can be seen from its extensive flood plain, it flourished as an important cross-Channel port until the 14th century. Its houses represent a diverse range of appealing architecture and styles, while the small museum, with Saxon and church relics, is definitely worth a call. Its Norman church, with a variety of surviving features, notably the impressive nave and its associated pillars and arches, was built by the abbey of Fécamp about 1150 and is well worth a look. The village is a first-class starting-point for bracing walks up on to the Downs, especially to **Chanctonbury Ring** and to Cissbury Ring.

Chanctonbury Ring (OS Grid Ref TQ139120) is one of the finest prehistoric hill-forts on the South Downs and commands exceptional views in all directions. Surrounded by the remaining beech trees planted by a local landowner in 1760, the ring also contains the site of a Romano-British temple and you can, apparently, raise the devil if you run around the rings seven times. The Norman church at nearby Buncton, containing recycled Roman building materials is worth a look.

Cissbury Ring (OS Grid Ref TQ140081) is the largest Iron Age fort in Sussex (80ac/32ha), built between 300 and 250 BC on the site of Neolithic flint mines and occupied down to the Roman era. It then became part of a cultivated Roman field system before being re-fortified in the 4th century as a defence against raiders from the sea.

Worthing is a busy sea-side and residential town that has 5 miles of shingle and sand seafront and a working pier. It grew up as a fashionable resort in the 18th century under the patronage of Princess Amelia, the younger and less flamboyant sister of the Prince Regent who favoured Brighton. However, despite a less intense and cosmopolitan character than Brighton, it does become congested in the summer months. It has a large number of parks and open spaces, mostly laid out in the Victorian and Edwardian eras. Boat porches are a unique architectural feature of Worthing; they frame the entrance doors of some early 19th-century houses, in the form of a stuccoed porch with an ogee-headed roof which looks like a boat. Oscar Wilde wrote *The Importance of Being Earnest* here, whose principal character is called Jack Worthing.

Worthing Museum and Art Gallery contains an interesting collection relating to the local history, geology and archaeology of the area, along with period costumes, pictures and toys, as well as a good collection of paintings by Sussex artists. Most importantly, it houses remains from the nationally significant Anglo-Saxon cemetery at Highdown Hill and from Cissbury, Harrow Hill and Blackpatch.

Down on the coast, between Worthing and Lancing is the remarkable Saxon church of **Sompting**. For most of the Middle Ages, the church was associated with the Knights Templar and, subsequently, the Knights Hospitaller, until that Order's dissolution in England in 1548. The nave dates from the 11th century and the transepts, which were added by the Templars, in the 12th century. Other major features include a 12th century doorway and font, as well as 13th century carvings on 11th century stones depicting Christ in Majesty and the symbols of the four evangelists. It is clear that all sorts of architectural features were recycled throughout the medieval period and the church is a treasure trove of items, both in their original setting and re-used, the most remarkable being the group of Saxon stones in the sanctuary.

However, its unique claim to fame and outstanding feature is its 11th century tower, 82ft/25metres high with walls 30inches/76cm thick, which has the earliest and only example of a four-sided pyramid 'Rhenish Helm' in England. The current supporting timbers are 14th century, but the construction of the tower shows that these replaced an earlier, similar

---

Worth Visiting

Marlipins is a 12th century house of Caen stone and flint that, after probably starting life as a hospice for travellers, was used as storage for wine and other goods. It was altered in the 14th century and today houses a first-class museum of local maritime, archaeological and agricultural antiquities, pictures and other curios.

Worth a look: Shoreham Airport is the oldest licensed airfield in Britain – with a revealing visitor centre/exhibition and guided tours for visitors and 'spotters'.

structure, which no doubt continued to appeal to the military ethos of the Hospitallers.

The 94 feet tall **Lancing College** chapel is spectacularly neo-Gothic and, although built from 1868, awaits completion. It contains canopied stalls brought from Eton College, tapestries made on William Morris looms and a 33ft/10m Rose Window.

Throughout its history, **Shoreham** has had to contend with the silting of the Adur and the close attentions of the sea. Old has given way to New Shoreham, which in turn has had to adapt to changing sea levels. Until 1804, the town was building warships and small trading vessels until the 1870s. Old Shoreham is the original port of Bramber, which has a Saxon and Norman church restored in 1840, but full of interesting details. North east of Shoreham, good views and walks are available from Mill Hill and beyond to Thundersbarrow Hill, where there are Iron Age banks and ditches, along with the remains of Romano-British lynchets and the traces of buildings.

Shoreham by Sea has a port that is still thriving today despite the fact that Adur enters the sea a mile further east. The working port with its long seaward spit running east-west is still thriving, with a brisk trade in leisure activity, fishing and aggregate extraction and export. Its most impressive feature is the remarkable church of St Mary de Haura (of the harbour), which dates from Norman times, when its nave was much bigger. It was modified throughout the medieval period, but five bays of its nave (the foundations are in the churchyard) were demolished in the 17th century. It is well worth the effort of an exploration.

North of The Downs

Just north of the Downs, **Henfield** is a large, sprawling village that is rapidly becoming a continuous urban development. The exhibitions in its museum are wide-ranging and informative about the local area. They include early fossils and implements, medieval and Tudor artefacts and a range of farming tools that would have been used to work the land in centuries gone by.

Horsham's origins are Saxon and the town grew into an agricultural market town in the Middle Ages, a status it retained well into the 20th century, although it also had thriving iron, brewing and brickworks industries. After extensive housing development and investment in Victorian times and during the 20th century (a past recalled by the photographs of Francis Frith), it is today a commuter and residential hub. Its local economy relies on financial services, technology enterprises and pharmaceuticals, although two small brewers still operate in the town. A good proportion of its heart is pedestrianised and flanked by shopping centres. It currently has a staunchly defended 'strategic housing gap' between itself and the constant threat of embrace by its rapidly expanding neighbour, Crawley.

Ifield Mill, Crawley

Worth Visiting

Buchan Country Park – two miles from Crawley, the park is 170 acres of woodland, heath and meadow that are suitable for walkers and children with energy to spare. With plenty of pathways, tracks, pools and streams, it is an accessible way of getting out of doors. Various sculptures have been positioned around the park and there is enough wildlife to go round.

Crawley Museum – a large collection of artefacts, photographs and pictures that relate to the local area.

Church of St Nicholas, Worth – a Saxon foundation, built between 950 and 1050, it suffered a disastrous fire in 1986 but was sympathetically rebuilt in 1988. Robert Whitehead, inventor of the modern torpedo is buried in the churchyard – his epitaph reads "His fame was known by all nations hereabouts".

Ifield – working water mill

Tulleys Farm – a farmers' outlet market that has various 'fun' rides, activities and mazes for families, as well as frequent seasonal events.

Worth Noting

In a timber-framed medieval house, **Horsham Museum** has over twenty-six galleries and two walled gardens that reflect local history and livelihoods. The rope for hangmen's nooses used to be made in Horsham.

The **Rising Universe Fountain** (erected to commemorate local boy made good, Percy Bysshe Shelley) on the western side of the town centre. The County Times said that it was 'a public work of art which has attracted widespread derision and distress' and Horsham's twin town, Lerici in Italy, called it 'very brave'. It is also unfortunate that modern water saving measures have meant that the supply to the fountain has been discontinued.

The **Old Town Hall** in the Market Square dates from about 1648 but today's much modified building of Portland Stone in 1721 was rebuilt in 1812 and, definitively, in 1888.

Crawley has traces of Roman and Saxon occupation and developed as a modest market town from the 13th century. The construction of a turnpike road between London and Brighton in 1770 and its position midway between London and newly fashionable Brighton made it a busy coaching stop. During the Victorian era and with the coming of the railways in 1848 (it had a railway works), it was a prosperous town that served a wide agricultural base and several local estates. In 1946, the New Towns Act designated Crawley as a New Town, to move people and jobs out of London, and rapid residential and commercial growth began, in step with plans for Gatwick Airport.

Its expansion since then has been continuous and dramatic, along with its rise in population. Modern Crawley hosts large numbers of service and light industrial companies and retail outlets, along with other high technology and engineering firms. Not surprisingly, nearby Gatwick Airport provides a significant amount of employment and service demand. The area is the main centre of industry and employment between London and the south coast and is continuing to expand.

Despite its almost universal modernity, there are a large number of listed buildings in and among the villages that have coalesced into greater Crawley, especially in Pound Hill, Worth and Ifield.

The site of **Gatwick** originally had a racecourse, built in 1890, that held the Grand National 1916-1918. The 1918 winner was Poethlyn ridden by E Piggott (Lester Piggott's grandfather). A private airfield was opened in 1930 on land near the racecourse, which subsequently operated commercial flights, but the site was taken over by the Royal Air Force during the Second World War. Its return to civilian use in 1946 and threats of closure eventually led to the development of London's second airport in 1958, with a second (North) terminal built in 1988.

Gatwick is the busiest single runway airport in the world, the second largest airport in the UK and the sixth busiest international airport in the world, with over 100 airlines flying to and from 200 destinations worldwide. It continues to expand and plans for a second runway and additional facilities are in train. Gatwick Aviation Museum – a small, enthusiastic aviation museum, with a collection of mostly British post-war aircraft and other memorabilia. It is normally open on Sundays only.

Horsham, Paninos Cafe

Buchan County Park

Horsham

Lancing College, Shoreham by Sea
Opposite: St Marys House Bramber

Below: **Crawley Museum**

Places to Visit

Bramber Castle
BN44 3FN west of Bramber off A283
www.english-heritage.org.uk
Open: daily in daylight hours

St Mary's House, Bramber
Bramber BN44 3WE
☎ 01903 816205
www.stmarysbramber.co.uk
Open: May-Sep, Sun, Thurs & BH Mons
2-6pm

Crawley Museum
Goffs Park House Old Horsham Road
Crawley RH11 8PE
☎ 01293 539088
www.crawleymuseum.moonfruit.com
Open: mid Feb-Oct, 2-4pm, Wed, Sat & BH Mon

Gatwick Aviation Museum
Vallance By-Ways Lowfield Heath Road
Charlwood RH6 0BT
☎ 01293 862915
www.gatwick-aviation-museum.co.uk
Open: 10am-4pm two Sundays per
month March-Oct.
Please check website

Henfield Museum
Coopers House Coopers Way Henfield
BN5 9EQ
☎ 01273 492507
www.henfield.gov.uk/museum
Open: Mon, Tues, Thurs, Fri, Sat 10am-
12pm; Wed, Sun 2.30-4.30pm. Closed
BH & Christmas

Horsham Museum
9 Causeway Horsham RH12 1HE
☎ 01403 254959
www.horshammuseum.org
Open; Mon-Sat, 10am-5pm

Ifield Watermill
Hyde Drive Ifield RH11 0PL
☎ 01293 539088
www.crawleymuseum.moonfruit.com
Open: May-Sep last Sunday of each
month & National Mills Day 2.30-5pm

Lancing College Chapel
Lancing College Drive Lancing BN15
0RW
☎ 01273 465949
www.lancingcollege.co.uk
Open: Mon-Sat, 10am-4pm, Sun &
BH 12-4pm

Marlipins Museum
36 High St Shoreham BN43 5DA
☎ 01273 463994
www.sussexpast.co.uk/marlipins
Open: Tues-Sat, May-Nov 10.30am-
4.30pm

Shoreham Airport Visitor Centre
Cecil Pashley Way Shoreham Airport
BN43 5FF
☎ 01273 441061
www.visitorcentre.info
Open: every day May-Sept, 10am-
5pm, telephone re winter opening

Steyning Museum
Church St Steyning BN44 3YB
☎ 01903 813333
www.steyningmuseum.org
Open: all year Tues, Wed, Fri and Sat
10.30am-12.30pm;
Tues, Wed, Fri, Sat & Sun, 2.30-
4.30pm Apr-Sep (4pm Oct-March)

Worthing Museum & Art Gallery

Chapel Road Worthing BN11 1HP

☎ 01903 204229 or 221448 (Sat)

www.worthing.gov.uk

Open: Tues-Sat, 10am-5pm

Country Parks, Farm Parks & Gardens

Buchan Country Park

South West of Crawley, off the westbound carriageway of the A2220

Grid Reference TQ245346

www.sussex.gov.uk

Highdown Gardens

Littlehampton Road Worthing BN12 6PG

☎ 01903 501054

www.highdowngardens.co.uk

Open: Apr-Sep, daily 10am-6pm; Oct-Mar 10am-4pm

Tulleys Farm

Turner's Hill Road Worth Crawley RH10 4PD

☎ 01342 715365

www.tulleysfarm.com

Open: daily Mar-Nov, 9am-6pm; Nov-Mar 9am-5pm

4. THE RAPE OF LEWES

Castle Lodge and Castle, near the Barbican, Lewes

Lewes is the county town of East Sussex. There is abundant evidence that the crossing over the Ouse was extensively settled by the Romans and fortified by the Saxons.

The town itself is strategically positioned at a point where the river Ouse flows through the chalk downs to the sea and where the great forest of the Weald ended. Important to the Romans and Saxons, it had two mints at the time of Edward the Confessor and was given to William the Conqueror's close ally, William de Warenne. He built the castle from 1078, probably on the site of a Roman fortification, and it was continually and substantially strengthened by his successors, resulting in the highly unusual arrangement (which it shares only with Lincoln Castle) whereby the site has two fortified mottes, or mounds. The view from the top is memorably spectacular.

The Barbican is a particularly fine example of mid-14th century military architecture and repays close attention, not least because it contains The Barbican House Museum and the Sussex Archaeological Society's archaeology collection, which in-

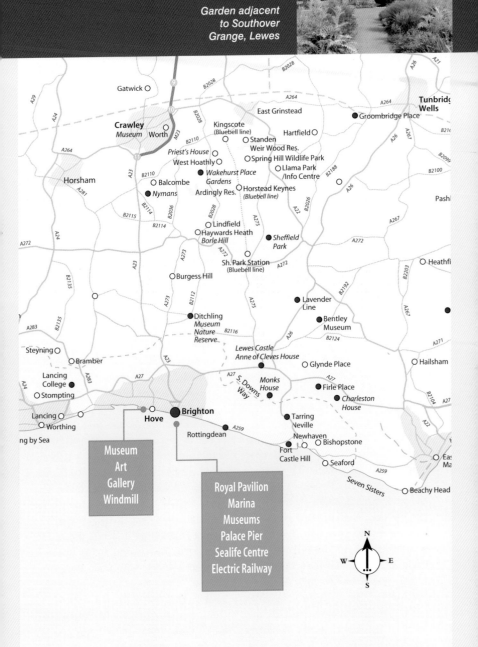

Garden adjacent
to Southover
Grange, Lewes

Gatwick

B2028

B2028

A29

A24

A264

East Grinstead

A264

Tunbridge Wells

Groombridge Place

A26

A21

B216

Crawley
Museum Worth

Kingscote
(Bluebell line)

Hartfield

Standen
Weir Wood Res.

A26

A267

B2099

A264

A23

B2110

Priest's House
West Hoathly

Spring Hill Wildlife Park

Llama Park
/Info Centre

B2188

B2100

Pashl

Horsham

A281

B2110

Balcombe

Wakehurst Place
Gardens

Horstead Keynes
(Bluebell line)

A26

Nymans

Ardingly Res.

B2115

B114

B2036

A272

B2026

A22

A24

A23

B2028

Lindfield
Haywards Heath
Borle Hill

A275

Sheffield
Park

A267

A272

Heathfi

B2114

Sh. Park Station
(Bluebell line)

A272

B2035

B2135

A273

A23

Burgess Hill

A275

Lavender
Line

B2192

A267

B2135

A283

A273

B2112

Ditchling
Museum
Nature
Reserve

B2116

Bentley
Museum

B2124

A271

Steyning
Bramber

A26

Lewes Castle
Anne of Cleves House

Glynde Place

Hailsham

Lancing
College
Stompting

A283

A27

S. Downs
Way

Monks
House

A27

Firle Place

Charleston
House

B2104

A27

A24

Brighton

A259

Tarring
Neville

A22

Lancing
Worthing

Hove

Rottingdean

Newhaven

Bishopstone

Eas
Ma

ng by Sea

Fort
Castle Hill

Seaford

A259

Beachy Head

Seven Sisters

**Museum
Art
Gallery
Windmill**

**Royal Pavilion
Marina
Museums
Palace Pier
Sealife Centre
Electric Railway**

N

W   E

S

cludes Iron Age, Romano-British and Anglo-Saxon displays. There is also 'The Story of Lewes Town' – a sound and light show based on a scale model of Lewes during the Victorian era and 'A Touch of Lewes' – an interactive touch-screen learning device.

The town grew in importance and as a significant port under the Norman kings and the battle of Lewes in 1264 was won nearby by the barons led by Simon de Montfort against the forces of Henry III. Later, between 1555 and 1557, seventeen Protestant martyrs were burnt at the stake in front of the Star Inn, now the Town Hall, during the reign of the Catholic queen 'Bloody' Mary. Iron, brewing and ship-building developed alongside the port in the 17th and 18th centuries before Newhaven's rise in the 19th led to the decline in Lewes' maritime status.

Parts of the town walls are still standing and much of the traditional street pattern survives, along with a variety of medieval plots and timber-framed buildings, most of which have more recent frontages. There are a number of good 18th century facades and several streets retain their 18th and 19th century cottages. Several houses have historic associations: Bull House was the home of Tom Paine (The Rights of Man) – now the headquarters of the Sussex Archaeology Society – and Anne of Cleves House, a Wealden hall house containing a museum, was given to the former queen as part of her divorce settlement by Henry VIII. A former windmill, the Round House in Pipe Street, was owned by Virginia Woolf. Along the river, Harvey & Son's Brewery, known as 'The Cathedral of Lewes' is a Victorian tower brewery which is the last of the town's major breweries still in business.

Lewes is known nationally for its exuberant and well-organised Bonfire Night, which celebrates Guy Fawkes Night on 5th of November and commemorates the seventeen Protestant martyrs killed under Bloody Mary. Often the occasion for major riots and major breakdowns in order in Stuart times, they were banned under the Commonwealth, but were revived in the 1840s. Despite a return to fighting and bad behaviour, they evolved, along with dedicated 'societies' parading in fancy dress, into the torchlight processions that are celebrated amid large crowds (up to 80,000) today.

Lewes Priory was founded by William de Warenne, lord of the rape of Lewes and earl of Surrey and his wife Gundrada in about 1081 and dedicated to St Pancras, a saint popular with the Saxons. It was the first Cluniac house in England and was sited in a commanding position on what was then the shore-line at the head of the Ouse valley. It had the largest church in Sussex and was longer than Chichester Cathedral, including its Lady Chapel.

At the Dissolution in 1537, the huge priory was demolished by an Italian engineer called Giovanni Portinari and the Prior's lodging was extended as a house for Thomas Cromwell's son. Major residential development took place from 1830, with many foundations and skeletal remains being cleared. In 1845, the London, Brighton and Hastings Railway drove their new line through the site, which cut through the foundations of the chapter house and church apse exposing the burials of, amazingly, of William and Gundrada de Warenne. However, much else was destroyed and the site was effectively divided. Even so, some fabric remains in Priory Field, which, although accessible, is fenced off pending preservation.

The Battle of Lewes in 1264 was the first of two battles between Henry III and Simon de Montfort in the conflict known as the Second Barons' War. The King was stationed at St. Pancras Priory with the royal infantry, while his son, Prince Edward (later King Edward I), leading the cavalry, was camped outside Lewes Castle, a mile away. De Montfort's forces surprised Prince Edward with a night approach and took the high ground of the Downs on Offham Hill. In the resulting battle, the King, his brother Richard of Cornwall and Prince Edward were captured. The site of the battle is to the west of the town, between Lewes Castle and the slopes of Offham Hill. It is marked at Priory Fields with a stunning monument by Enzo Plazzotta, which was erected on the 700th anniversary of the battle in 1964 and is in the shape of a 13th century helm decorated with graphic scenes from the battle of Lewes.

Pelham House dates back to the sixteenth century and features architecture of all subsequent eras and a private landscaped garden facing the Downs. It now serves as an independent hotel. Shelleys Hotel is likewise of some antiquity with a private garden and family associations with Percy Shelley.

Worth a look

One of the best municipal gardens in Sussex is **Southover Grange Gardens**, with the 16th century Grange at its heart, built of sandstone from the site of the dissolved Lewes Priory.

Nearby is the **church of St John the Baptist**, originally built in the 12th century as the hospice at the gate of the Priory of St. Pancras. It was converted into a parish church and has a nave and chancel, with an aisle and a modern section that houses the Gundrada Chapel. The arcade of the aisle is 12th century, but much other work is apparent from 14th-16th century. The Gundrada chapel contains the remains of William and Gundrada de Warenne.

Nearby are:

Stoneywish Nature Reserve has 50 acres of meadows and ponds, a wildlife walk, animals and a good place for families to enjoy picnics and walks together.

The **Barlow Collection** is one of the most important collections of Chinese ceramics in Britain. At the University of Sussex, it displays a comprehensive exhibition of Chinese history and culture.

Monk's House, between Lewes and Newhaven, was the second home of

One of the oldest buildings in Lewes can be found in the main street

***The Barbican**, Lewes*

*A **Russian** cannon, Lewes Castle*

Monk's House, Rodmell, former home of Virginia Woolf

Newhaven Fort

the novelist Virginia Woolf and her husband Leonard. The 18th century weather-boarded cottage was bought by the Woolfs in 1919 and rapidly became associated with visits by the Bloomsbury Group, including T S Eliot, E M Forster and Lytton Strachey. Virginia's sister, the artist Vanessa Bell, had lived at nearby Charleston Farmhouse in Firle since 1916. Virginia Woolf used to write her novels in the wooden building in the garden during breaks from London and, from 1940, to escape the Blitz, the Woolfs lived at Monk's House all the time until Virginia drowned herself in the river Ouse in 1941. Leonard remained until he died in 1969. The house was given to the National Trust in 1980 and is furnished as it was in 1969, with mementoes and lots of photographs of the Woolfs' life there.

Newhaven, at the mouth of the River Ouse, was already settled during the Iron Age, at Castle Hill, and is an international ferry port, running services to Dieppe. The 18th century village of Tide Mills contains old cottages and a historic tide mill and the museum has an interesting collection of exhibits, model boats and maritime photographs and archives. **Newhaven Harbour** is underrated and has opportunities for exploring the beach under the cliffs or enjoying the activity and entertainment available around the haven. The modern marina has added extensive facilities and a touch of style to the harbour area, with space for 300 boats.

Newhaven Fort, built in the 1860s, is the largest fortification in Sussex, with extensive ramparts, gun emplacements and tunnels. It has an impressive collection of militaria and reminders of life in the fort over the past 150 years – and beyond.

The fourteen hectare Castle Hill (OS Grid ref TQ 442003) nature reserve overlooks the English Channel and has been set aside for wildlife to flourish. The area is a site of special scientific interest and is also known for its colonies of kittiwakes and fulmars.

Paradise Park has exotic plants and a worthwhile museum of natural and local history. 'Treasures of Planet Earth' exhibits flora, fossils and minerals, as well as dinosaurs. The gardens form part of the Sussex History Trail and the dinosaur's terrain, replete with moving dinosaur robots and suitable noises.

St Michael's Church dates from the 11th century and was used as a lookout to cover the harbour during the World Wars. The destroyer *Brazen* sailed from here and was sunk. A memorial to the ship's company is in the graveyard.

Across the river and technically in the rape of Pevensey, St Mary's in **Tarring Neville** is a delightful 13th century church, which has Grade 1 historic status and some notable medieval features.

Heading West to Brighton

To the west, past the inexorable coastal ribbon development of Peacehaven, Saltdean and **Rottingdean** (honourable mention to St Margaret's church which contains Burne-Jones stained glass and his ashes), the eminence, size and popularity of

Brighton has overshadowed its twin town of **Hove** to the west. The two communities form a continuous urban and beach-front mass along the seafront, with a 7 mile esplanade that stretches from Rottingdean through Hove and Brighton to Portslade and beyond in the west.

At the time of Domesday Book, Brighthelmston was a large fishing village (which owed a rent of 4,000 herrings in 1086), but, despite having 80 fishing boats and 10,000 nets in the 15th century, did not thrive because of the advance of the sea and periodic raids by the French. Amid fluctuating economic fortunes in the 16th and 17th centuries, Charles II escaped from Brighton after his defeat at the battle of Worcester in 1651. It was not until 1754, when Dr Richard Russell of Lewes promoted sea-bathing and a mineral spring at Hove as the means by which ailments and various conditions could be alleviated or cured, that the place started to grow significantly. Thackeray in *Vanity Fair* wrote about 'Kind, cheerful, merry Doctor Brighton,

The Prince of Wales, who later became Prince Regent and George IV, first visited the town in 1783 and his patronage ensured that this increasingly popular destination (about 6 hours by coach from London) would continue to expand as a leading leisure and health resort. He lived here with his (secret) first wife Mrs Fitzherbert in a summer house, enlarged by Henry Holland in 1787. Forced by his debts and the danger of losing the succession to the throne, he married Caroline of Brunswick in 1795, but returned to Brighton to be with Mrs Fitzherbert until he became Prince Regent in 1811 and the relationship ended. The Prince continued to visit the increasingly fashionable town until 1827 and had his villa – now the Royal Pavilion – rebuilt by John Nash 1815-22 in a fantastic Oriental style. Mrs Fitzherbert remained – discreetly – in Brighton until her death in 1837, when she was buried at the Catholic (a clue to why she was a problem for Prince George) church of St John on Bedford Street. Note her effigy, with three wedding rings.

Early in the 19th century, with a very speedy and efficient coach service from London, the town became the major cross-Channel ferry port. The subsequent arrival of the railway in 1841 ended the ferry trade, but meant that Brighton, with its many Regency terraces and squares, became even more accessible to day and weekend trippers, particularly Londoners, culminating in the mass tourism of the 20th century.

Today, Brighton, with over 150,000 inhabitants, has a cosmopolitan and exotic feel to it and its social scene is decidedly lively, with many clubs and entertainment outlets catering to each and every taste. It is a town that is full of surprises and worth exploring in detail, whether along the Esplanade, in a maze of old streets or when simply looking up at the host of handsome Regency and Victorian buildings, especially Royal Crescent, built 1798-1807 and Regency Square (Landseer's house – he of 'The Monarch of the Glen' and the lions in Trafalgar Square). The extensive gardens, lawns and flower-beds are a distinctive feature of the town.

The historic heart of Brighton is Old Steine, an open space with gardens near the Palace Pier where fishermen

The Royal Pavilion, *Brighton*

The **Sealife Centre**

Lindfield, *near Haywards Heath*

The Priest's House, *West Hoathly*

used to dry their nets and which is still partly surrounded by fine houses built in the 1780s. Mrs Fitzherbert lived at number 55 and the unspoiled late 18th century houses at 44-46 are worth a look in passing. Another old quarter is **The Lanes**, a closely packed network of streets that is famous for its antique shops, alternative merchandising and trendy pubs and restaurants. North Laine (www.northlaine.co.uk) is another, more eclectic mix of streets that hosts over 300 alternative and original shops and establishments in half a square mile. Also worth a look are the large numbers of fine art dealers and galleries in which Brighton seems to excel. However, in July and August, these areas, as well as the Esplanade and the King's Road, are positively 'heaving' and full of visitors.

The **Royal Pavilion** began life as 'a respectable farmhouse' and was converted into a fashionable villa by Henry Holland 1788-95, with some Chinese interiors fitted in 1801. The Royal Stables and Riding School were built in 1803 in the Islamic style of India, which made a considerable impression on the Prince of Wales. Consequently, as Prince Regent, he commissioned John Nash to complete the building in its present configuration and style, with its distinctive spires, domes, colonnades and minarets and Chinese interior decoration 1815-22. It was described at the time as 'this terrestrial paradise ... the most original, unique and magnificent structure in Europe'. Hazlitt, less impressed, called it 'a collection of stone pumpkins and pepper-boxes'.

After George IV's death in 1830, the Pavilion received visits by William IV and Queen Victoria, but after the latter decided to build and holiday at Osborne in the Isle of Wight in 1845, the fittings were removed and the furniture taken to Buckingham Palace. The Pavilion was acquired by the town in 1850 for £53,000 and used (appropriately) as a hospital for injured Indian soldiers. Since 1936, it has been progressively and sympathetically restored and, today, its sumptuous rooms contain the borough's notable collection of period furniture, pictures and fittings, as well as those loaned by the Royal Collection and others. The décor, interiors and style are quite unlike anything else in the county – or country – and the building should not be missed. The Dome, originally the royal stables, was converted into a concert hall in 1867 and then used as part of the war-time hospital from 1914-20, before finally being transformed into a theatre, complete with a dual-purpose concert organ.

Other significant attractions

The parish church of **St Nicholas** dates from the 14th century and contains a beautifully carved Norman font. Among many interesting memorials, one is to Captain Tettersall who helped Charles II to escape and who was liberally rewarded as a result. Another commemorates Martha Gunn, once of the most famous Regency 'dippers', or bathing attendants. Finally, there is Phoebe Hessell who served in the Army for 17 years to be with her man and fought at the battle of Fontenoy – and lived to the age of 108.

Brighton Marina – was built from 1971-7 and opened as the biggest marina in Europe in 1978 to howls of local protest (out of character, ugly, not in my back yard etc). To no-one's surprise, the original project went way over budget and this led to the progressive residential and commercial development of the site. Today, it is a vibrant, popular complex of flats and houses, retail outlets, restaurants and bars representing the usual marina entertainment leisure amenities and trendy opportunities to spend money.

Brighton Museum & Art Gallery – in the Pavilion grounds, the modern museum houses nationally important collections of Fine Art (over 2000 paintings and other exhibits from around the world) and Fashion Design, as well as dedicated galleries, interpretation sequences and exhibitions relating to the history and life of Brighton, its people and its local area.

Booth Museum of Natural History – an exhaustive collection of birds in their natural habitats, skeletons and lots of butterflies, with 'hands-on' opportunities.

Volks Railway – from 1883, the world's first public electric railway, it runs from the Palace Pier to Black Rock (one and half miles to the east).

Palace Pier – built in 1891-9, the pier gives an interesting promenade out over the sea (1722 ft), has fairground attractions and houses the National Museum of (!) Slot Machines. The West Pier, built in 1866 and 1150 ft long in its day, is derelict. (There are plans to build a 360 degree observation tower)

Preston Manor – a Georgian House built in 1739 on Tudor foundations, with decorated rooms, which contains the Thomas-Sandford collection of furniture, silver, china and a library of books on Sussex.

Sea Life Centre – The original aquarium opened in 1872, with 'commodious tanks'. Today's equivalent has over 150 species and over 50 displays, including close-up experiences with sharks and turtles above an underwater tunnel. Various habitats from around the world are reproduced, inhabited by exotic creatures, such as the Amazon Rainforest and Serpents of the Sea which has sea snakes, eels and other wriggly things. Good for families and children, when not crowded.

Toy and Model Museum – under the railway station, contains a large collection demonstrating how toys have evolved over centuries, with over 10,000 toys, models, computers and trains. There is also a great shop.

Theatre Royal – built in 1806, the venue offers a range of professional productions all year round.

Further afield:

The Chattri (OS Grid Ref TQ304110) – this elegant memorial was erected in 1921 on the site of the burning ghat of those Sikh and Hindu servicemen who died as a result of their injuries in the First World War and had been hospitalised at Brighton. It is on the Downs, about a mile from Patcham.

Ditchling Beacon (OS Grid Ref TQ333130) dominates this section of the South Downs ridge and is the site of an Iron Age fort, with a single defensive bank and ditch enclosing an area of about 13.6ac/5.5hectares. Beacon Road, which is steep and narrow, gives access to the top of the hill, where there is a car park administered by the National Trust. A decent walk from Hassocks railway station along footpaths is an alternative, as are summer buses from Brighton.

Two excellent walks are available from Ditchling Beacon, both offering excellent views: one follows the South Downs Way westward to Bramber, while the other takes in Standean and Stanmer, with views of Mount Caborn and the Firle Gap, and has the opportunity to press on to Mount Harry or Lewes.

The village of **Ditchling** lies at the foot of the South Downs and has two Sites of Special Scientific Interest - Ditchling Common (heath grassland) and the Clayton to Offham Escarpment (chalk grassland, woodland and scrub habitats). It also has a museum devoted to the local community's history and archaeology.

Hove

Hove is Brighton's quieter sister, a distinctly residential and occasionally elegant district, with parks and gardens and is the home of Sussex County Cricket Club. Importantly, Hove Beach is a mile-long stretch of sand whereas Brighton has a primarily stony beach. The Kingsway is the continuation of Brighton's King's Road and walkers will immediately sense the difference in tone. The houses and gardens in Brunswick Square are particularly appealing – a naval officer serving in

HMS Victory at the battle of Trafalgar, George Augustus Westphal, lived at no. 2.

Hove is home to the **British Engineerium**, a working steam museum that has a huge collection of full-size and model engines, as well as tools and other historic technology. At the time of writing it is temporarily closed but opening dates can be checked on www.britishengineerium.com. **The Hove Museum and Art Gallery** has themed Georgian, Regency and Victorian rooms, as well as a Sussex Room (local History), an Archaeological Room (mostly Romano-British) and a Children's Room (Toys and dolls). It has an extensive collection of ironwork, porcelain and pottery, together with glass, silver and other curios.

West Blatchington Windmill. – Built on a brick and flint tower, this 'smock' (because it looks like one) mill dates from the 1820s, with all its machinery intact and working on five floors. Visitors can learn about traditional milling techniques and view other agricultural exhibits.

Behind Hove are **Devil's Dyke** (a huge V-shaped cleft in the Downs – OS Grid Ref TQ258110) and **Fulking Hill** (OS Grid Ref TQ247114), both of which offer stunning views and an energy-sapping, challenging climb on foot, if undertaken all the way from Hove. A good ridge walk is available westward and then southward to Edburton Hill and beyond, to Truleigh Hill and Thundersbarrow Hill. Both are prehistoric settlement sites. Another great walk leads west to Beeding and Steyning along the South Downs Way (as above) and continues to Chanctonbury and Cissbury Rings. To the north, **Haywards Heath** is a rapidly expanding urban, commuter and commercial hub at the centre of the rape that will soon swallow up Burgess Hill and Hurstpierpoint, both to the south. It had been a small, heathland village until the railway arrived in 1841 – the proposed route through Cuckfield had been rejected by local landowners. However, it is a convenient transport link and base for expeditions into the High Weald and there are good walking routes in all directions to the north. As for **Burgess Hill**, a local guide says it all, 'there aren't many obvious visitor attractions in **Burgess Hill**'.

However, just to the east of Haywards Heath is **Sheffield Park Gardens**. Laid out by the eminent landscape gardeners Humphrey Repton and Capability Brown in the 18th century, and then further developed in the early 20th century by Arthur Soames. Amid spectacular parkland, there are four ornamental lakes that were probably hammer ponds which provide depth and contrast to the spectacular, shimmering arrays of plants, trees and shrubs. The National Trust owns the house (Tudor, but remodelled as a Gothic mansion by James Wyatt for John Baker Holroyd, first earl of Sheffield, in 1779) and 200 acres of parkland. Between 1884 and 1896, the cricket pitch was the venue for the opening match of any Australian XI tour, until the event moved to Arundel. The invitation team included W G Grace. Edward Gibbon, the author of the *Decline and Fall of the Roman Empire*, who died while visiting Sheffield Park, is buried in the church of the nearby village of Fletching.

One of the most vibrant and exciting volunteer projects in Sussex is the **Bluebell Railway**, a heritage line that runs steam trains for nine miles between Sheffield Park and Kingscote, with an intermediate station at Horsted Keynes. The Bluebell Railway was the first preserved standard gauge steam-operated passenger railway in the world when it opened in 1960, shortly after the line from East Grinstead to Lewes was closed. An extension to East Grinstead is currently under way and the Bluebell Railway has purchased the track bed of the abandoned line between **Horsted Keynes and Ardingly**.

It has an outstanding collection of steam locomotives, which is the largest in the UK after the National Railway Museum (NRM), and almost 150 carriages and wagons. There is a regular service daily and the stations have been restored to represent railway life at various stages in the line's history.

Towards the north, **Ardingly** is the site of the Royal Agricultural Society Showground and the South of England Agricultural Show. **Ardingly Reservoir** was completed in 1978 after 198 acres of land along the course of the River Ouse was dammed. Today, the lake is a local beauty spot, with a wide variety of flora and fauna, including large numbers of resident and migratory birds and freshwater fish. There is a footpath along the east bank and opportunities for yachting and canoeing.

Close by, **Balcombe** has a viaduct that allowed the London to Brighton railway to span the valley of the River Ouse; it was completed in 1842, stretches for almost 500 metres and contains 11 million bricks. The viaduct was restored in the 1990s and has Grade II* listed status.

Nearby Gardens

There are four magnificent Wealden gardens in the vicinity of Ardingly: **Borde Hill** is set in over 200ac/81ha of traditional park and wood land, with, at its heart, a Tudor mansion of 1598 and a 17ac/7ha garden, largely created in the Edwardian era and which flourishes all year round. It has magnificent views across the High Weald, but its speciality is a range of champion (tallest or largest girth) trees in England and exotic plants from around the world, as well as a distinctive series of 'living garden rooms' and various woodland walks.

High Beeches is a very attractive landscaped woodland garden of 20ac/8ha, whose paths and trails take visitors through very varied plant collections and cleverly designed landscapes, punctuated by waterfalls and pools. It includes the National Collection of Stewartia Trees and what is supposed to be the finest natural wildflower meadow in Sussex. High Beeches House was destroyed by fire when an aircraft crashed into it during the Second World War.

Nymans reflects the considerable dedication of the Messel family from 1892 onwards. The Regency house, modified to resemble a 14th century building in the 1920s, was gutted by fire in 1947. The remaining rooms were patched up and used as family home and base from which to develop the gardens, but, in 1953, Nymans became one of the first gardens to be transferred to the National Trust. The 30ac/12ha garden itself is positioned on the side of a valley and is laid out as a series of rooms and levels connected by stone steps or grass approaches – notably the Wall Garden (the oldest), the Knot Garden, the Rose Garden, the Top Garden, the Sunken Garden and the Pinetum. The gardens contain many unusual designs and an abundance of rare and exotic species. The remaining Messel family apartments, including 17th furniture and Flemish tapestries, are open to the public.

Wakehurst Place Garden is owned by the National Trust and, since 1965, has been managed by the Royal Botanic Gardens, Kew. Set in 465ac/188ha, it is usually the Trust's most visited attraction and has an extremely pleasant and intriguing mixture of walled and water gardens, together with more natural woodland and wetland conservation areas. It also houses the Millennium Seed Bank Project (preserving 10 per cent of the world's species and still going) and a very informative interactive exhibition. Wakehurst has the largest growing Christmas tree in England, at 115ft/35m tall; it is lit with 1,800 lights from Advent until Twelfth Night. The Mansion was built in 1590.

To the east, at West Hoathly, the **Priest House** is an early 15th century timber-framed hall building. After being owned by Lewes Priory, Thomas Cromwell and Anne of Cleves, the house came into the Browne family. Its arrangement of open hall, with a solar, upper chamber and service end was extended to include stone chimneys and two additional rooms upstairs, as well as a Horsham stone roof. The house and its contents were given to the Sussex Archaeological Society. Today, the house contains 17th and 18th century furniture and other domestic items and has a formal herb garden.

Places to Visit

Booth Museum of Natural History
194 Dyke Road Brighton BN1 5AA
☎ 03000 290900
www.brighton-hove.gov.uk
Open: daily except Thurs, 10am-5pm & Sun 2-5pm. Closed Good Friday, Christmas & New Year

Brighton Museum and Art Gallery
Royal Pavilion Gardens Brighton BN1 1UE
☎ 03000 290900
www.brighton-hove.gov.uk
Open: Tues-Sun, BH Ms 10am-5pm. Closed Christmas & New Year

Brighton Palace Pier
Madeira Drive Brighton BN2 1TW
☎ 01273 609361
www.brightonpier.co.uk
Open: 9am until midnight in the summer; 10am until midnight in the winter

Brighton Royal Pavilion
Pavilion Buildings righton BN! 1EE
☎ 03000 290900
www.royalpavilion.org.uk
Open: Oct-Mar, 10am-5.15pm; Apr-Sep 9.30am-5.45pm.
Closed 24-26 Dec

Brighton Sealife Centre
Marine Parade Briughton BN2 1TB
☎ 0871 4232110
www.sealife.co.uk
Open: daily from 10am-5.30pm; Sat & Sun 6.30pm

Brighton Toy and Model Museum
52-55 Trafalgar Street Brighton B N1 4EB
☎ 01273 749494
www.brightontoymuseum.co.uk
Open: Tues-Sat, 10am-5pm; 4pm on Sat

Preston Manor
Preston Drive Brighton BN1 6SD
☎ 03000 290900
www.brighton-hove.gov.uk
Open: Apr-Sep, Tues-Sat, 10am-5pm; Sun 2-5pm

Volks Electric Railway
Marina Drive Brighton N2 1EN
☎ 01273 292718
www.volkselectricrailway.co.uk
Trains run daily in the summer season

Wakehurst Place Gardens

The Barlow Collection

Library Building University of Sussex Falmer Brighton BN1 9QL
☎ 01273 873506
www.sussex.ac.uk/barlow
Open: Tues & Thurs 1- 4pm. Closed during university vacations

Elsewhere

Crawley Museum

Goffs Park House Old Horsham Road Southgate Crawley RH11 8PE
☎ 01293 539088
www.crawleymuseum.moonfruit.com
Open: mid Feb-Oct, Wed, Sun & BH Mons, 2-4pm

Ditchling Museum

Church Lane Ditchling BN6 8TB
☎ 01273 844744
www.ditchling-museum.co.uk
Open: May-Oct, Tues-Sat & BH Mons, 10.30am-5pm (2-5pm on Sun)

Grange Art Gallery and Museum

High Street Rottingdean BN2 7HE
☎ 01273 301004
Open: every day except Wed

Hove Museum and Art Gallery

19 New Church Rd Hove BN3 4AB
☎ 03000 290900
www.brighton-hove.gov.uk
Open: Tues-Sat, 10am-5pm; Sun 2-5pm & Closed Christmas & New Year

Lewes:

Anne of Cleves House

High St Lewes BN7 1JA
☎ 01273 474610
www.sussexpast.co.uk/anneofcleves
Open: Mar-Oct, Tues-Thurs 10am-5pm; Sun, Mon & BH 11am-5pm; closed Fri & Sat

Lewes Castle & Barbican House Museum

169 High St BN7 1YE
☎ 01273 486290
www.sussexpast.co.uk
Open: Tues-Sat 10.30am-5.30pm & 11am on Sun & BH Mons

Monk's House

Rodmell Lewes BN7 3HF
☎ 01323 870001
www.nationaltrust.org.uk/main/w-monkshouse
Wed & Sat 2-5.30pm

Newhaven Fort

Fort Rise Newhaven BN9
☎ 01273 517622
www.newhavenfort.org.uk
Open: daily March-Oct 10.30am-6pm (5pm in Oct)

Newhaven Local & Maritime Museum

Paradise Park Avis Road Newhaven BN9 ODH
☎ 07760 713422
www.newhavenmuseum.org.uk
Open: daily Apr-Oct, 2-4pm (5pm on Sat Sun & BH); Nov-Mar, Sat & Sun only 2-4pm

Nymans - House
Handcross Haywards Heath RH17 6EB
☎ 01444 405250
www.nationaltrust.org.uk
Open: mid-March to Oct, Wed-Sun BH
Mons; Nov-Feb; closed Christmas/New
Year

The Priest House
North Lane West Hoathly RH19 4PP
☎ 01342 810479
www.sussexpast.co.uk
Open: Mar-Oct, Tues-Sat 10.30am-
5.30pm & from 12noon on Sun

West Blatchington Windmill
97 Holmes Ave Hove BN3 7LE
☎ 01273 776017
www.sussexmillsgroup.org.uk/open2.
htm
Open: May-Sep, Sun, BH & National
Mills & Heritage Sunday 2.30-5pm

Gardens
Borde Hill Garden
Haywards Heath RH16 1XP
☎ 01444 450326
www.bordehill.co.uk
Open: daily from late March to mid-Sept
& last week in Oct 10am-6pm

High Beeches
High Beeches Lane Handcross RH17
6HQ
☎ 01444 400589
www.highbeeches.com
Open: late March-Oc,t daily except
Wed 1-5pm

Nymans
Handcross Haywards Heath RH17 6EB
☎ 01444 405250
www.nationaltrust.org.uk
Garden open all year, Wed-Sun and BH
Mondays

Paradise Park
Paradise Park Avis Road Newhaven
BN9 ODH
☎ 01273 512123
www.paradisepark.co.uk
Open: daily 9am-6pm,
closed 25 &26 Dec

Sheffield Park Gardens
Sheffield Park TN22 3QX
☎ 01825 790231
www.nationaltrust.org.uk
Open: daily mid-Feb to Oct, 10.30am-
5.30pm
Open: weekends Jan to mid-Feb; Nov &
Dec 10.30am-4pm; closed 24-27 Dec

Southover Grange Gardens
Southover Road Lewes BN7 1UF
☎ 01273 483448
www.lewes.gov.uk/business/11757.asp
Open: daylight hours

Wakehurst Place Gardens & Millenium Seed Bank
Selsfield Road, Ardingly RH17 6TN
☎ 01444 894000
www.kew.org/visit-wakehurst
Open: daily except 25 & 26 Dec, 10am-
6pm Mar-Oct & 10am Nov-Feb

left: **Eastbourne Pier**
below: **Pevensey Castle**

The stretch of coast between Seaford and Eastbourne is the Sussex Heritage Coast, incorporating spectacular scenery and the eastern end of the South Downs Way. Seaford, which was, originally, the major port of the rape of Lewes at the mouth of the Ouse, had the misfortune to find itself in the rape of Pevensey when a storm diverted the course of the river to Newhaven in 1579. With a beach that shelves steeply away, it is still at risk both from erosion and from westerly gales which throw shingle and water over the sea wall – hence the massive wooden groynes on the beach.

Seaford to Eastbourne

On the front is a **Martello Tower**, the most westerly of a chain of similar lookout and defensive strong points, 103 of which were hastily erected between **Seaford** and Aldeburgh in Suffolk to counter the threat of invasion by Napoleon in 1803-15. 43 are still standing and Seaford's is an informative museum. The impressively big and ancient church of St Leonard has a history back to 1090. It was extended in the 12th century to cope with a growing population. Much of the original medieval structure survives, along with fine architectural detail and stained glass windows from later times.

St Andrew's church, in the really pretty village of **Bishopstone** – a short distance from Seaford – has claims to be the oldest surviving Saxon church in Sussex (having been built between AD 600 and 800). This wonderful church has recently been sensitively restored, revealing its Saxon and Norman detail and many other early features.

To the east, Seaford Head is host to a 300ac/121ha Nature Reserve (OS Grid Reference TV510976) that includes Cuckmere Haven (canoes and boats permitted) and part of the river valley. There are numerous paths that enable visitors to explore, as well as access to rock pools and river, which at the haven can only be reached on foot

through water meadows; the one to Hope Gap affords the best view of the **Seven Sisters**.

The undulating chalk sea-cliffs of the Seven Sisters are the quintessential view that everyone has in their mind when they–erroneously–think about the white cliffs of Dover. Amid spectacular views, the **Seven Sisters Country Park** comprises 700ac/280ha of chalk cliffs, river valleys and open chalk grassland and balances opportunities for a range of outdoor activities, along bridleways and tracks and along the sea-shore, with the need for nature conservation and sustainability. There is an interpretation centre at Exceat, in a group of converted flint barns. Inland, the 2000-acre Friston Forest is leased to the Forestry Commission and offers a range of way-marked routes, with fine views, all the way, to Wilmington or East Dean, and its church with a Norman tower whose walls are 3 feet thick. On the coast, the next feature is Birling Gap, with cottages and a café overlooked by an Iron Age fort on Lookout Hill.

Beachy Head (from the Norman-French Beau Chef) is the highest point on the Sussex coast – at 534ft/163m and rises sheer from the rock-strewn foreshore. There is a nature trail and a small natural history centre open during weekends in summer. Well below, the lighthouse is 142 ft high; the base of its predecessor, built in 1834, is on the cliff top, a mile and a half to the west.

Eastbourne

Eastbourne was developed by the 7th Duke of Devonshire from about 1850 and the coming of the railways saw it grow into a thriving resort. Its accommodation and amenities constantly try to keep pace with demand from tourists, residents and retired people alike. The extensive beach is mostly shingle, but is sandy at low tide. Eastbourne Pier was built in 1870, but, in 1877, the landward half was carried away. It was rebuilt at a higher level, creating a slope towards the end of the pier. You might not want to know that the pier is built on stilts resting in cups on the seabed, allowing the whole structure to move during rough weather.

Eastbourne has plenty of the usual English sea-side entertainment and leisure opportunities, as well as a range of – sometimes quirky – museums: a Museum of Shops – the 'How we lived Then' Museum and the Royal National Lifeboat Institution Museum. The progressive Sovereign Harbour Marina Development has the usual berthing and boating amenities, as well as thousands of apartments and houses, bars and restaurants, a large out of town shopping centre close by and a six screen cinema.

At the eastern end of town is the **Redoubt Fortress** which was built 1804-10 at the eastern end of the town and manned by up to 350 troops, to complement the Martello towers. It needed 5 million bricks to construct the 24 casemates which are arranged in a ring placed in a ring 220ft/67m in diameter. The moat is 25ft/7.6m wide and 24ft/7.3m deep but could never be filled because the fortress was standing on shingle. The only entrance was across a bridge to the landward face of the fortress; the seaward face was reinforced with concrete. On the front is a Martello, called the **Wish Tower** (from the Anglo-Saxon wisc meaning 'marshy site') and it contains a good museum about the Martello system.

Worth seeing/doing

The **Cuckoo Trail** is an excellent 14-mile (23 km) footpath and cycleway which runs along an old railway track from Hampden Park, Eastbourne to Heathfield, passing through Horam, Hailsham and Polegate, and forming part of National Cycle Network Route 21.

The new **Towner Art Gallery** – with a collection of 4000 historic, modern and contemporary works.

Sussex Voyages in Sovereign Harbour – guided trips in rigid-hulled inflatable boats to Beachy Head, the Seven Sisters and the Royal Sovereign Light Tower, as well as fast sea-rides.

The **Military Museum of Sussex** in the Redoubt Fortress

Eastbourne Heritage Centre – well-researched local sea-side history

Eastbourne Miniature Steam Railway – good fun on one-eighth scale locomotives and rolling stock around a one-mile country circuit!

Pevensey

Originally built on a peninsula at the mouth of a small river on the coast, **Pevensey Castle** is now far from the sea, although the channel was still navigable until 1700. It has the unusual distinction, with Portchester (in Hampshire), of being a Roman fort (Anderida) that has a Norman castle within its walls. The 10ac/4ha, unusually oval, site was fortified at the end of the 3rd century, as part of a chain of forts (the Saxon Shore) that defended the coast against raiders and attacks from the sea. In the sub-Roman period, in 491, it witnessed a notable massacre of Britons at the hands of the invading Saxons, as recorded in the Anglo-Saxon Chronicle and was abandoned.

After the Norman invasion and the battle of Hastings in 1066, an earth and timber castle was built inside the fort by Robert, Count of Mortain, with a stone keep added in 1100 and the rest of the massive present stone structures were erected in the mid- 13th century. It played a notable part in the power struggles of the medieval period and underwent several sieges, but, by Tudor times, was already ruinous and obsolete. It was briefly occupied by Canadian and United States Army Air Force personnel in World War II and was given anti-air defences. Today, the castle is a fascinating mix of Roman and medieval survivals and its many interesting features and evocative position looking out over the levels make it a very rewarding site

to explore in detail, especially with inquisitive children.

The village of **Pevensey** is built on the site of the original Roman and Saxon harbour where William of Normandy was supposed to have landed in 1066 and was a powerful member of the Cinque Ports confederation in the Middle Ages, that is, before the sea retreated. Its church is mainly 13th century and is worth a look. **Pevensey Courthouse Museum** is housed in the old 16th Century courthouse on the High Street and tours of this building are available, which show visitors the history and development of Pevensey, a variety of artefacts and the two prisoner's cells in the courthouse itself. To the north-east, Pevensey levels are an expanse of gloomy marsh and rivulets once covered by the sea.

Near **Polegate**, the church in the attractive village of **Wilmington** is predominantly medieval and was part of a priory founded in the 11th century. Its ruins, that have successively been a farmhouse and a vicarage, can be seen amid later buildings to the south of the church. The buildings on the site now house an agricultural museum. The feature that people instinctively associate with Wilmington is the 226 ft/69m high **Long Man**, whose origins are obscure, but certainly less risqué than the shameless Cerne Abbas Giant in Dorset. Explanations range from a representation of a Norse god (possibly Baldur) to an innovative way of alerting pilgrims on the route to and from Winchester and Chichester to Canterbury to the fact that accommodation was available at the priory. Whatever its origins, the man retains his outline because white bricks were inserted in Victorian times.

Wilmington Forest is a large area of protected woodland just a few miles to the north of Eastbourne in the beautiful East Sussex countryside. It is recognised as a great place to go for a stroll and particularly if you are interested in seeing unusual wildlife and plant life. The forest has several tracks through it and is popular in the summer months.

The picturesque **Arlington Reservoir 1.25mile/2km** (OS Grid Ref TQ535075) has a route around the Osprey Trail, with hides to allow bird watching. Arlington church is also worth a call – it is Saxon by origin and has incorporated recycled Roman materials. Incongruously, the village is home to the **Eastbourne Eagles** speedway team and banger racing at the Arlington Stadium! **Polegate Windmill** was built in 1817 and spent over a century in service. The mill is open to the public and visitors can see the inner workings of the machinery.

Alfriston

Just before Alfriston is the very popular and imaginative **Drusillas Park**. This is an adventure park and zoo combined, with plenty of themed rides and activities, primarily for children up to the age of 13. Always busy, it can be expensive over a whole day, especially for food and extras.

Alfriston itself, with traditional cottages, houses and shops, built around the Market Square and its weathered cross, is a highly photogenic, very commercialised and much visited village, nestling at the foot of the Down and overlooking the river Cuckmere. Wooden figures front the Star Inn, which was originally a pilgrim hostel built in 1345, but became an inn after the Reformation in the 16th century. The church of St Andrew on a small mound on the 'tye' – or village green – was a Saxon foundation, although the present cruciform structure was built in 1360, and is known as the 'The Cathedral of the South Downs'.

Another St Andrew's is a non-conformist United Church, which was founded in 1801 and has gallery pillars made from recycled ships' timbers. A real gem is the **Alfriston Clergy House**, a 14th-century Wealden hall house, which was the first property to be acquired by the National Trust in 1896 for £10. It is a low-ceilinged, two-storey, timber-framed building with a thatched roof, designed to house a priest and a housekeeper.

On the A27 east of Lewes, **Charleston** is a country house that was strongly associated with the Bloomsbury Group, reflecting from 1916 the work of Vanessa Bell (Virginia Woolf's sister) and Duncan Grant; with over sixty years of artistic endeavour and creativity. The Woolfs, Lytton Strachey and John Maynard Keynes were frequent guests, as were other members of the group. The influence of Italian fresco painting and the Post-Impressionists can be seen in the decoration of the walls, doors and furniture, while the garden

Eastbourne Pier

Charleston Farmhouse, off the A27 near Alciston

Alfriston

comprises mosaics, box hedges, gravel pathways and ponds, as well as statues. The collection includes work by Renoir, Picasso, Derain, Matthew Smith, Sickert, Tomlin and Delacroix. Visitors can see the house, with its murals, furniture and products from the Omega workshops, and garden, together with an exhibition gallery and a Bloomsbury Group themed art and book shop.

Two grand houses, both in striking situations amid the hills, are well worth a visit, when you can: **Glynde Place**, built in 1569, but remodelled in 1752 now has a Georgian appearance and an extensive collection of important paintings and bronzes. The nearby opera house of **Glyndebourne** was built in 1934, now supplemented by a newer, bigger brick and steel edifice and enjoys considerable favour and popularity with the aesthetic community. **Firle Place** was built in 1471 and was also altered considerably around 1730. It contains a substantial collection of English and French furniture and paintings by noted Old Masters, including Fra Bartolomeo, Rubens and Reynolds. The restored medieval church in the village of **West Firle** has several monuments of the Gage family, the owners of Firle for over 500 years.

Above Glynde, a good walk will reach another commanding view and a long-lost Iron Age settlement on **Mount Caburn**. The fort had a single bank and ditch, with a double ditch on the side of easiest approach; the site proved so useful that it was re-fortified after the Romans left and again during the civil wars of Stephen's reign.

At Bentley, the **Wildfowl & Motor Museum** is home to a wide variety of native and exotic water birds, as well as over 100 vintage and classic cars and bikes. The elaborate gardens take in a woodland trail, an adventure playground, a steam mini-railway and the usual amenities for a day out.

The **Raystede Centre for Animal Welfare**, near Ringmer, is a worthy cause and a good family visit, with over 1,000 animals, including horses, pigs, exotic birds, ducks and domestic pets. Over 1,500 unwanted and abandoned animals arrive at the centre annually and are found suitable homes, while others remain in care.

A little further up the Ouse, **The Lavender Line** is a one mile long heritage line, complete with locomotives and rolling stock that operates trains every 30 minutes from Isfield towards Little Horsted. The station at Isfield has been well restored and offers a range of train-based activities and amenities, including food and drink, a model railway and a working signal box.

Moving rapidly back to the eastern side of the rape, there are two different types of 'experience' near **Hailsham**: The delightful fortified priory of **Michelham** dates back to 1229 when it was founded by Augustinian canons and has the largest water-filled moat in England. The story of Michelham is told in its 'Island of History', including its dissolution under Henry VIII in 1537 and the destruction of its church of the Holy Trinity. As a private house and estate, the priory underwent selective demolition, incorporation of various monastic buildings, including the prior's lodging, and modification, which included the addition of a 16th century wing. The collection of objects and architectural features in the house reflect its long life as a priory, working farm and country estate. The gatehouse, built in 1395, and bridge across the moat are impressive.

There is evidence that milling took place at least as early as 1434 and on the estate there is a water mill, which is used for producing flour for sale and use in Priory-made produce. A hands-on grinding and milling experience with querns is available. Also on site are: a working forge (when the blacksmith is there); a rope museum; an Elizabethan Great Barn (1590s); an Iron Age Centre with a roundhouse and other primitive replica buildings and a play and picnic area.

Meanwhile, the 80ac/32ha **Knockhatch Adventure Park** has a wide range of indoor and outdoor activities that will appeal to children of all ages – crazy golf, quadapillar barrel rides, boating, go-karts and all the usual stuff to let off steam. There is a bird of prey centre, reptiles and various animals too.

Crowborough does not seem to have much to recommend it as it is a commuter and residential town, except for a charming miniature railway on the approach road to the town's leisure centre. The small-gauge railway has signals, a station house and a large boating lake. The trains run in summer and on most Sundays. Don't overlook the walk up to Crowborough Beacon - and the view.

To the north

East Grinstead is situated in the north of the rape and on the Greenwich Meridian. It has been an important market town since the 13th century and was for a long period a centre for Wealden iron working. Today East Grinstead is one of more prosperous towns in Sussex, with a proportion of residents commuting to London. Its centre and conservation area have several historic properties including a long continuous sequence of 14th century timber-framed buildings in the High Street. There are also several boutiques, specialist shops and arts and crafts outlets, as well as the normal civic amenities. The town has a modern, particularly attractive museum that has a well-presented and fully interpreted collection of artefacts, documents and exhibitions relating to local history and town life, as well as paintings and sketches by local artists.

The building of **Standen** in 1890, to the south, was commissioned by James Beale, a successful London lawyer, and his wife who bought a group of farm buildings on the hillside site now occupied by the house. They invited Philip Webb, a friend of William Morris to design and supervise the building of the house and its interior, having seen examples of his work in London. The result is a modest late-Victorian house that blends well with its surroundings, incorporating the existing farm buildings and using the materials and architectural style of the original 15th century farmhouse which is connected to the main house by a covered archway. The buildings are

Worth a look:

Sackville College was founded in 1609 as an almshouse and is one of the best preserved Jacobean buildings of its type in Sussex. Around a quadrangle, the sandstone college provides sheltered accommodation for the elderly and remains faithful to its original principles. The popular carol 'Good King Wenceslas' was written here by the then warden the Rev Dr John Neale. The Grade I listed building is open to the public.

grouped around a village green, with a large courtyard area at the rear of the house. Not surprisingly, the interior is a wonderful advertisement for the **Arts and Crafts** movement, with its stress on the balanced combination of nature and architecture, and for the various textiles and soft furnishings of William Morris and his company.

As well as embroidery by Mrs Beale and her daughters, the house contains some of the best examples of William Morris wallpaper in the country and the fabrics, carpets, ceramics and furniture are by a range of leading personalities in the Arts and Crafts Movement. The property still has its original electrical light fittings.

There is a fine conservatory featuring Edwardian houseplants as well as a beautiful cultured garden to explore, designed, on advice, by Mrs Beale. The many paths give exhilarating views of the High Weald and the surrounding area.

To the south and east, **Ashdown Forest** covers over 6,400ac/2590ha of the High Weald and there are considerable opportunities for exploration, walking or riding along a network of paths and bridleways. The best place to start is the Ashdown Forest Information Centre (OS Grid Ref TQ433323), which has a wide selection of detailed maps and ideas. There are over fifty car parks around the forest, as well as picnic areas. Look for The Ashdown Forest

Worth a look:

East Grinstead Clock Tower was first erected on a building, which has since been demolished, in 1890, but was restored and re-sited in 2000.

Victoria Hospital Museum – a museum that tells the story of the hospital, and its connection with the armed forces. It has an extensive photograph archive and historic equipment from the hospital on display.

Saint Hill Manor was the home of L Ron Hubbard, the founder of the Church of Scientology and is the headquarters of the church today. It is a very fine late 18th century sandstone building which stands in 60 acres of grounds that can be explored. It also has an intriguing collection of furnishings, curios and antiques, reflecting a fascinating blend of Eastern and Western cultures.

Firle Place (Images courtesy Firle Place)

Llama (and Alpaca) Park – animals in an outdoor parkland area with a visitor centre, gift shop and a well-appointed café and snack bar.

Further east, **Hartfield**, lying on the northern edge of Ashdown Forest, is the location of Cotchford Farm, the home of A A Milne, author of the *Winnie the Pooh* books. All the 'Enchanted Places' including the famous 'Pooh-sticks Bridge' can be found in the parish. The village shop, built in the 17th century, has the largest collection of 'Pooh-phernalia' in the world.

In the far north of the rape is **Groombridge Place**. In 1239, a moated castle was authorised on the site and the estate passed through the Russell, de Cobham and Waller families. In 1618, the house was sold to the Packers by Sir Thomas Sackville, earl of Dorset and, by 1662, Groombridge was in the hands of an architect, John Packer, who built the current house and laid out the gardens, with the help of Christopher Wren and John Evelyn. This caused him financial difficulties and, apart from serious trouble with smuggling in the 18th century, the house has had an uneventful history for much of the past 350 years. Today, it is in private ownership and is not open to the public. However, the gardens, set in 200ac/81ha, are available to view and are based on a series of delightfully arranged, traditional walled gardens, using the moat and manor house as a backdrop. Highlights include the 'Enchanted Forest', the so-called 'Drunken Garden' (the favourite garden of Sir Arthur Conan Doyle, who set his Sherlock Holmes story, the *Valley of Fear* at Groombridge) and, on the hill slopes, a range of modern gardens. Also, there

is a Raptor Centre, with flying displays by birds of prey, canal boat trips and restrained fun for children.

The **Spa Valley Railway** (SVR) is a 4mile/6.4km long standard gauge heritage railway, started in 1996, that runs between Tunbridge Wells, High Rocks, Groombridge, and Birchden along the former Three Bridges to Tunbridge Wells Central Line / Cuckoo Line. The line is currently being extended to Eridge.

Right in the north-eastern corner of the rape and in the Wealden country on the border of Sussex and Kent, **Bewl Water** is south-east England's largest lake. It offers facilities for walking and cycling (cycles are available for hire), including a 13mile/21km 'Round Water Route', water sports and angling, as well as the ability to cruise on a passenger boat amid wonderful scenery. Children can also enjoy a woodland adventure playground and rides.

Bayham Abbey is about as close to the border with Kent that it could be, along the valley of the river Teise. It was built of local sandstone in the early 13th century by Premonstratensian canons and was extended in the 15th century, particularly through the rebuilding of the transepts of the abbey church. In 1538, it was among the first monasteries to be dissolved and was leased initially to Sir Anthony Browne, although it passed into the Pratt family by 1714. Their descendants used the abbey ruins as a picturesque feature within a landscaped estate (by Humphrey Repton and recorded in his *Red Books*) centred on the family residence of Bayham Old Abbey House. In 1872, the Camdens, the successors to the Pratts, moved across the river to Bayham Abbey

House and the ruins passed to the care of the state in 1961. Today, the ruins are maintained by English Heritage and well worth seeing. Despite the robbing of stone, many walls remain to indicate the outlines of the various buildings and there are decorated capitals and other carved work still in place.

Places to Visit

Alfrston Clergy House

The Tye Alfriston Polegate BN26 5TL
☎ 01323 870001
www.nationaltrust.org.uk
Open: every day Mar-Oct, 10.30am-5pm except Tues and Fri; open Good Fri & Fri in Aug;
Nov-mid Dec, 11am-4pm, every day except Tues and Fri

Ashdown Forest Llama Park

Wych Cross Forest Row East Grinstead RH18 5JN
☎ 01825 712040
www.llamapark.co.uk
Open: daily 10am-5pm; closed 25 & 26 Dec and 1 Jan

Bayham Abbey

OS Grid Ref TQ651366
Postcode: TN3 8DE
2miles west of Lamberhurst off B2169
☎ 01892 890381
www.english-heritage.org.uk
Open: daily Apr-Sept 11am-5pm

Bentley Wildfowl & Motor Museum

Halland Nr Lewes BN8 5AF
☎ 01825 840573
www.bentley.org.uk
Open: Mid-March to Oct 10.30am-5.30pm
House opens daily at noon Apr-Oct

Bewl Water Reservoir

Bewlbridge Lane Lamberhusrt TN3 8JH
(Sussex/Kent Border)
www.bewl.co.uk
Open: daily from 9am until sunset; closed Christmas Day

Charleston

Firle Lewes BN8 6LL
☎ 01323 811265
www.charleston.org.uk
Open: Apr-Oct, Wed-Sat 1-6pm;
Sun & BH Mons 1-5.30pm

Drusillas Park

Alfriston Road Alfriston BN26 5QS
☎ 01323 874100
www.drusillas.co.uk
Open: 10am-6pm during British summertime, otherwise10am-5pm
Closed 24-26 Dec

Eastbourne:

Eastbourne Heritage Centre

2 Carlisle Road Eastbourne BN21 4BT
☎ 01323 411189
www.eastbournesociety.co.uk
Open: mid-Apr to Sep 2-5pm

*The **Court House and Museum**, Pevensey*

Pevensey Castle

Eastbourne Lifeboat Museum

King Edwards Parade Eastbourne
BN21 4BY
☎ 01323 730717
www.eastbournernli.org.uk/
Eastbournelifeboatmuseum.
Open: daily Apr-Oct 10am-5pm;
Oct-Jan & Mar 10am-4pm; Jan & Feb
Sat & Sun 11am-2pm

Eastbourne Miniature Steam Railway

Lottbridge Drove Eastbourne BN23 6NS
☎ 01323 520229
www.emsr.co.uk
Open: daily 10am-5pm, end of March to
beginning of Oct & some Oct weekends

Museum of Shops and Social History

20 Cornfield Terrace Eastbourne
BN21 4NS
☎ 01323 737143
www.sussexmuseums.co.uk/how_we_
lived_then.htm"
Open: daily from 10am, closing times
vary. Please call to check

Redoubt Fortress & Military Museum

Royal Parade Eastbourne BN22 7AQ
☎ 01323 410300
www.eastbournemuseums.co.uk
Open: Apr-Oct, Tues-Sun & BHs,
10am-5pm

Towner Contemporary Art Museum

Devonshire Park College Road
Eastbourne BN21 4JJ
☎ 01323 434670
www.eastbourne.gov.uk
Open: Tues-Sun, 10am-6pm

East Grinstead Museum

Cantelupe Road East Grinstead
RH19 3BJ
☎ 01342 302233
www.eastgrinsteadmuseum.org.uk
Open: Wed-Sat, 10am-4pm, Sun & BH
2-5pm. Closed over Christmas

Firle Place

Firle, Lewes, BN8 6LP
☎ 01273 858307
www.firleplace.co.uk
Open: June-Sept Sun, Wed, Thurs,
Easter Sun & BH Mons 2-4.15pm

Glyndebourne Opera

Lewes BN8 5UU
☎ 01273 812321
www.glyndebourne.com
For tickets and events please see
website

Glynde Place

Glynde Place BN8 6SX
☎ 01273 858224
www.glynde.co.uk/glynde_place
Open: May-August, Wed, Sun and BH
Mons 2-5pm (guided tours only)

Knockhatch Adventure Park

Hailsham Bypass Hailsham, BN27 3GD
☎ 01323 443051
www.knockhatch.com
Open: daily Apr-Aug and weekends in
Sept & Oct, 10am-5.30pm
Check website for winter opening times

Michelham Priory

Upper Dicker Hailsham BN27 3QS
☎ 01323 844224
www.sussexpast.co.uk/michelham
Open: Tues- Sun, Mar-Oct
10.30am-5pm

Pevensey Castle

Pevensey BN24 5LE
☎ 01323 762604
www.english-heritage.org.uk
Open: daily Apr-Sept 10am-6p;, Oct
10am-4pm; Nov- March 10am-4pm,
weekends only

Pevensey Courthouse Museum

High St Pevensey BN24 5LF
☎ 01323 762309
www.pevenseycourthouse.moonfruit.
com
Open: May-Sept, Mon-Sun 10am-5pm

Polegate Windmill

Park Croft Polegate BN26 5LB
www.sussexmillsgroup.org.uk
Open: Easter-Oct, 2-5pm; Sun & BH
Mon in Aug

Saint Hill

Saint Hill Road East Grinstead
RH19 4HY
☎ 01342 326711
www.sainthillmanor.org.uk."
Open: all year daily tours of the house
on the hour 2-5pm. Closed 25 & 26 Dec
& 1 Jan

Seaford Museum

The Esplanade Seaford BN25 9BH
☎ 01323 898222
www.seafordmuseum.co.uk
Open: Easter-Oct Wed & Sat 2.30-
4.30pm; Sun & BH 11am -1pm &
2.30-4.30pm;
Nov-Easter Sun & BH 11am-1pm &
2-4pm

Standen

West Hoathly Road East Grinstead
RH19 4NE
☎ 01342 323029
www.nationaltrust.org.uk
Open: Mid-March to Oct, 11am-
4.30pm, Wed-Sun & BH Mons

GARDENS

Groombridge Place Gardens

Groombridge Hill Groombridge
TN3 9QG
(Sussex/Kent Border)
☎ 01892 861444
www.groombridge.co.uk
Open: Apr-Oct 10am -5.30pm or dusk
if earlier. Please check times

Sheffield Park Gardens

(for description see the Rape of Lewes)
Sheffield Park TN22 3QX
☎ 01825 790231
www.nationaltrust.org.uk
Open: daily mid-Feb to Oct, 10.30am-
5.30pm; weekends Jan to mid-Feb,
Nov & Dec 10.30am-4pm. Closed
24-27 Dec

COUNTRY PARKS & ANIMAL CENTRES

Raystede Centre for Animal Welfare

Ringmer BN8 5AJ
☎ 01825 5AJ
www.raystede.org
Open: daily 10am-4pm

Seven Sisters Country Park

Exceat Seaford BN25 4AD
☎ 01323 870280]
www.sevensisters.org.uk

Seven Sisters Sheep Centre

Gilberts Drive East Dean BN20 0AA
☎ 01323 423302
www.sheepcentre.co.uk
Open: Mar-Apr for lambing; July-Aug for sheep milking & shearing,
2-5pm weekdays; 11-5pm weekends and school holidays

The Long Man of Wilmington

Windover, Wilmington
Access to the base of the figure
24 hours a day, 365 days of the year
www.sussexpast.co.uk

BOAT TRIPS

Sussex Voyages

Sovereign Harbour Marina Eastbourne
BN23 6JH
☎ 0845 8387114
www.sussexvoyages.co.uk
For sailing dates and times please check website

RAILWAYS

Bluebell Railway

– see description in the Rape of Lewes
Sheffield Park Station TN22 3QL
Horsted Keynes Station RH17 7BB
☎ 01825 720825
www.bluebell-railway.co.uk
For timetable and events see website

The Lavender Line

Isfield Station Nr Uckfield TN22 5XB
☎ 01825 750515
www.lavender-line.co.uk
For timetable see website

Spa Valley Railway

West Station Tunbridge Wells TN2 5QY
☎ 01892 537715
www.spavalleyrailway.co.uk
For timetable see website

The most easterly of the Sussex rapes, the coast of this part of the county has been continuously shaped by changes in coastal topography over the centuries and partially marred by unsympathetic 20th century ribbon development, the area between St Leonard's and Bexhill (the so-called Costa Geriatrica) being a typically unsatisfactory example. Further inland, life is rural, quiet and agricultural, a legacy of the great forest of the Weald, which dominated life on the border between Kent and Sussex. However, it has often been at the forefront of English national life, through both warfare and trade, and several of the great events of English history have occurred along the strip of coast that faces onto the Continent, in particular Normandy.

Left: **Batemans (NT)**
Right: **Bodiam Castle (NT)**

Tunbridge
Wells

A76
A21
A228
B2162
B2079
A229
A274
A21
A21
A262
A262
B2169 ● Bayham Abbey
A26
A267
● Scotney Castle
B2099
B2100
● Nat. Pintum
Bewl Water
B2086
B2100
A229
A268
B2099
A28
● Pashley Manor
Gardens
A268
K & ES Railway
Etchingham ○
● Great Dixter
○ Hurst Green
○ Northiam
A265
● Bodiam Castle
B2244
○ Bateman's
A268
○ Heathfield
○ Brightling
A21
B2203
B2096
B2089
○ Rye
Winchelsea
Museum ○
○ Camber
Castle
A267
A2100
A28
● Windmill Hill
● Battle
Abbey 1066
A271
B2204
A259
○ Guestling
B2204
B2095
● Herstmonceux
Castle
A2100
B2095
A259
○ Hailsham
A259
Hastings
B2104
● Bexhill
A27
○ Pevensey
A22
A259

○ Eastbourne
Marina

○ Beachy Head

N
W E
S

Castle
Lifeboat Station
Museums (2)
Shipwreck Heritage Centre
Smugglers Adventure
Blue Reef Aquarium
West & East Cliff Railways

In the west of the rape, **Herstmonceux** is notable for its impressive 15th century brick-built and elegantly moated castle, set within extensive parkland and gardens, alongside some incongruous astronomical domes. Built as a residence rather than as a fortress from 1441, its interior was demolished in 1777, but completely rebuilt in 1933 to house a variety of English and French styles. The castle and its Elizabethan gardens are open to the public.

After occupation by the Admiralty in 1946, the grounds became in 1957 the headquarters of the Royal Greenwich Observatory (close to the Prime Meridian) until its move to Cambridge in 1988. Several telescopes remain in the grounds and the Newton Telescope and the Equatorial Telescope Buildings have been converted to the **Observatory Science Centre** an interactive, hands-on experience that, with its outdoor Discovery Park and over 100 space-themed exhibits, will greatly appeal to children. Today, the castle and grounds also house the Bader International Study Centre, for undergraduates studying various aspects of International Law. Just to the east, the village of **Windmill Hill** is named after the windmill located on its highest point. Built in 1814, the Grade II listed building is a fine example of the classic post mill, which is occasionally opened to the public.

Moving down to the coast, **Bexhill** is a seaside resort, shopping centre and dormitory town whose most interesting landmark is the **De La Warr** (pronounced Delaware, like the US state) Pavilion, built in the International style in 1933-6. Often mistaken for an Art Deco design, passers-by might reflect on two comments made about the building:

> *"Delighted to hear that Bexhill has emerged from barbarism at last, but I shall not give it a clean bill of civilisation until all my plays are performed there once a year at least."*
> **George Bernard Shaw.**
>
> *"A fine modern building with absolutely no architectural merit at all. It was opened just in time to be bombed. The plane that dropped it was said to have been chartered by the Royal Institute of Architects..."* **Spike Milligan.**

Hastings

Hastings' modern drabness, down at heel appearance and commercial uniformity belie its substantial heritage and considerable interest for the visitor. Originally, it is likely that it was a Roman settlement and military outpost, before being occupied by the followers of a Dark Age chieftain called Haesten, hence its original name of Haestencester. An important late-Saxon town, it was incorporated as the head of the Cinque Ports under Edward the Confessor and reached its heyday as a trading and cross-Channel port under the Norman and Angevin kings (roughly 1066-1204). Successive silting, inundations by the sea and frequent French raids after the loss of Normandy in 1204 and during the Hundred Years' War led to the progressive decline of the port.

By the 18th century, the town was known for its boat-building, fishing and smuggling, before the arrival at the end of the century of significant numbers of people seeking restorative cures and recreation by the sea-side. This trend was accelerated by the increased mobility afforded by the railway which arrived in 1851 and various attractions were centred on the pier built in 1872 but damaged by fire in 2010. The town then thrived as a holiday and beach resort up until the 1950s and, today, its extensive beach is still thronged by hotels of various types, the usual sea-side attractions, parks and gardens, as well as, from spring to early autumn at least, seasonal and day trippers. Access to and from the cliff-tops is by flights of steps, lifts or the **West Hill Cliff Railway,** a funicular giving access to the castle and St Clement's Caves.

The best, most attractive part of Hastings is the 'Old Town', which adjoins the area of beach known as the Stade (from the Saxon meaning 'a landing place'). Fishing boats are still drawn up onto the beach and the Stade retains traditional tall timber sheds, used to house nets and tackles that occupied the least possible surface area in order to avoid taxes. Nearby is an interesting, popular **Fishermen's Museum** housed in a chapel of 1854. The Old Town itself is centred on All Saints Street and the High Street and is a pleasant jumble of houses of differing styles and antiquity that is well worth exploring.

Amid the half-timbered and other period houses and shops, buildings of note are the *Old Count House*

(1425), *Pulpit Gate* (at the bottom of All Saints Street), the *Piece of Cheese* and *Shovells* (the family home of the admiral Sir Cloudesley Shovell, who was wrecked and died on The Scillies in 1707). The **Old Town Museum** tells the story of Hastings in the past and the 15th century All Saints church is worth a look. It was originally built soon after the Norman invasion, but in 1339 it was ruined by a French raid on the town. It was rebuilt in the 15th century at the bequest of Richard Mechynge who left money in his will to restore the church to its original design.

The numerous alleys that run off the High Street and are known locally as *twittens* are worth exploring in detail. St Clement's church, just off the High Street, dates from the late 14th century and its tower contains cannonballs fired by passing French warships in the 1720s. The pre-Raphaelite, Dante Gabriel Rossetti married Elizabeth Siddal here in 1860.

The steps nearby lead to St Clements Caves (and the hands-on attraction **Smugglers' Adventure**), three acres of underground passages and galleries, said to have been used by smugglers and extended in Victorian times, and to the scant, but dominant remains of the castle. The site of William the Conqueror's first wooden castle, the present structure was started by Robert Count of Eu, between 1068 and 1080, and re-built by Henry III, before coastal erosion and its use as a quarry by the locals led to its current condition by the 16th century.

Nevertheless, a visit will be rewarded, not just for its historical associations (including an audio visual experience

The Stade, Hastings

The **Shipwreck and Coastal Heritage Centre** *(left)* &
The Blue Reef Aquarium *(right)*

of the castle and the Conquest), but also for first-class views of the *Stade* and the Old Town.

Pelham Crescent at the base of the hill on which the castle stands, along with the classical church of St Mary-in-the-Castle, are good examples of Regency design. Opposite on East Hill, is **Hastings Country Park** (520 acres), which runs for 5 miles along the coast and comprises woods, heath and watercourses, and offers some of the most rewarding walking in Sussex. It can be accessed by East Hill Cliff Lift.

Inland and a good way from Hastings (4miles/6.4km), **Battle** has a cluster of buildings originating from the medieval period, notably the timber-framed Pilgrim's rest near the Abbey, and from the 17th and 18th centuries. It is the site of the memorable and decisive battle of Hastings in 1066, one of the most famous dates in English history, where William, Duke of Normandy, defeated King Harold II, to become king of England and earn his familiar title 'the Conqueror'. The features of the battlefield are still recognisable today, despite the imposing ruins of the huge abbey founded by William on the crest of Senlac Hill where the English army was positioned and Harold was killed. A detailed interpretation centre, museum and well sign-posted walk around the battlefield and abbey make for an instructive, fascinating and thought-provoking tour (as long as the site is not too crowded). You will want to ask yourself why it was that William chose to charge his cavalry

Also worth a look:

The **Old Town Hall Museum** in the High Street houses a collection of objects and documents about the history of the town and the area.

The Blue Reef Aquarium – the usual local eco-system and species approach.

Hastings Museum and Art Gallery – an unusual collection of Native American, Asian and Australian exhibits, as well as wildlife galleries.

Hastings Lifeboat Station and Visitor Centre – a look at the Mersey Class boat and a guided tour.

Shipwreck Heritage Centre – a collection of what has washed up locally over hundreds of years.

The Fishermen's Museum – in an old church provided for seamen in the mid 19th Century and gives a view of the history of fishing, with paintings, documents and artefacts.

up what even today is a distinctly steep hill and whether the official Norman accounts hide the fact that he might have caught Harold by surprise. The abbey itself is a vast ruin that easily repays a detailed exploration, especially the gatehouse (built in 1338 against the French) which contains a very instructive, highly accessible exhibition of antiquities and interpretation panels.

Around Hastings

In the early medieval period, East Sussex was covered by native woodland, which was subsequently cleared for iron-working and farming. However, the 200-hundred acre **Battle Great Wood** (OS grid reference TQ762159) remains, managed by the Forestry Commission and covers nearly two hundred acres and is a fantastic place to walk, ride and discover the diverse plant and animal life in the wood.

Brightling, also near Battle, has several unusual buildings, including a large structure known as Fuller's Tower. The 35 ft tower was built, along with the other follies in the village, by 'Mad (see Bodiam) Jack' Fuller in the 1820s. It can be reached by a footpath and visitors can climb to the top to see a tremendous view. Jack Fuller's distinctive pyramid mausoleum can be seen in the churchyard. In addition, he built, on one of the highest points in the South Downs, the Brightling Obelisk, or Needle. At 646ft/197m above sea level, it is the second highest point in East Sussex and is thought to commemorate either (only Mad Jack would know) the Battles of Trafalgar or Waterloo.

Moving along the coast to the east, **Guestling** is one of the county's prettiest villages and is located roughly half way between Hastings and Rye. At the heart of Guestling is the very attractive parish church of St Laurence, which was Saxon, with Norman towers and stained glass windows. The stone carvings both inside and outside are worth a good look.

Winchelsea & Rye

Highly competitive trade and corporate rivals, but staunch partners in the struggle against the French during the early medieval period,

---

Also worth a look in Battle:

Yesterday's World – set in a medieval hall house, this attraction is social history with a difference, comprising walk-through and interactive audio-visual displays, as well as a huge number of authentic artefacts and several recreated contexts, portraying life from the Victorian period to the 1950s.

St Mary's Church – originally Norman (1110-25), the building has been remodelled in the 12th century and again in 1869, but has several rewarding features and memorials, including that of Sir Anthony Browne, (a leading courtier of Henry VIII) for those who like to explore and reflect. Within the village, Caldbec Hill (or Kingsmead Open Space) is where King Harold rested his troops on the night before the battle and gives access to walkers and outstanding views across the South Downs.

the delightful towns of **Winchelsea** and **Rye** occupy isolated hills at the southern ends of two sandstone fingers that reach down towards the sea and are separated by the River Brede. The towns face each other at a distance of only a mile and a half across a marsh that used to be a wide sea harbour and have been the backdrop for artists that have included Turner (The Blind Girl) and Millais. The poet, Coventry Patmore, said, 'Winchelsea is a town in a trance, a sunny dream of centuries ago; but Rye is a bit of the old world living pleasantly on, in happy ignorance of the new'. Visitors might reflect that both places are very much aware of how the locals – albeit pleasantly - are able to combine the romance of the past with the savvy commercialism of the modern age!

The original town of **Winchelsea** lay two miles to the South East of the present town. Two great storms of 1252 and 1288 finished off the old town, which had already suffered from coastal erosion. The inhabitants had planned for this eventuality and a new town was constructed from 1272 on Iham Hill based on a grid-iron fortified town plan from Gascony.

Many of the houses have underground crypts used for storing casks of wine and other goods. Despite the move, it maintained its prosperity and was one of the more powerful Cinque Ports, as it was at the junction of three rivers and was the primary port for the iron, wool and other products coming out of the Weald, and a considerable importer of wine from Gascony. However, like Rye, it was often attacked and sacked during the Hundred Years'

War at a time when the Black Death was raging and the sea was receding. By the Tudor period, it was stranded a mile inland and its port and trading links were no longer viable. It became a classic 'rotten borough' until the Great Reform Act of 1832.

Much of the original area of the planned town was never occupied and the town walls have disappeared. However, the town gates are well worth a visit, as they are typical of the late 13th century and have inspired several artists, including Turner. The Strand Gate (the most complete) has four drum towers and two archways (as well as views over Romney Marsh), while the positions of the New Gate (a mile away from the town) and the Pipewell or Land Gate, both repaired in the reign of Henry V (1413-22), show how large the new town was planned to be. Hogs Hill windmill near New Gate was erected at Pett in 1670, but moved to its present site in 1790.

Built at about the same time as the gates and not to be missed is the church of St Thomas the Martyr, a fine example of the Decorated Style of the High Middle Ages. It was probably planned to be much bigger and in cruciform shape, but its prospects inevitably dwindled with those of the town. Only the chancel with its aisles (the present nave) and a ruined transept remain today, as the original nave and two western towers have disappeared. Nevertheless, it holds some intriguing tombs and memorials, including that of Gervase Alard, the first to hold the title of Admiral of the Cinque Ports in 1325, reflecting the importance of the town. The Alards were a leading

Also worth a look:

Court Hall – built in the late 13th century, much restored and used as the town gaol, or Water Bailiff's Prison, the building now houses the perky town museum. Here, for the past 700 years every Easter Monday, the mayor and *jurats* of Winchelsea have been elected.

Winchelsea Beach is actually nearer Rye and is a sandy beach that stretches for around four miles in each direction.

Also worth a look:

Lamb House – in West Street, former home of E F Benson, Rumer Godden and Henry James. Owned by the National Trust, but, although the house and gardens are impressive, the house does not have many literary mementoes.

Rye Art Gallery – the Stormont Studio combines a selection of 19th and 20th century British art, including work by local artists, with the Easton Rooms, a 'Crafts Council Listed' gallery exhibiting and selling a wide range of work by local artists and craftspeople.

Rye Castle Museum – situated in the Ypres Tower and on East Street, the museum tells, as you would expect, the story of Rye.

The Rye Heritage Centre – on Strand Quay, this includes the sound and light Story of Rye, the Rye Town Model and the restored Old Sail Loft, as well as a gift shop.

Chapel of the Augustinian Friars – a medieval ruin, on Conduit Street.

Town Hall – built in 1743 and containing some interesting exhibits in passing.

Victorian Rye Windmill is a distinctive landmark that repays a close look, even though it is today a bed and breakfast establishment!

family of wine merchants and ship owners whose commitment to the new town had been vital. Millais' famous painting *L'enfant du Regiment* was painted inside the church, using one of the tombs.

Rye is possibly the most picturesque town in the county, with its irregular cobbled streets, medieval character and half-timbered buildings. Positioned on the River Rother and a member of the Cinque Ports since 1191, it received its charter in 1289 and its town wall and Landgate were erected in 1329. It prospered when Hastings was inundated and Winchelsea destroyed by a huge storm in 1287. It suffered severely from the Black Death and cross-Channel raiding throughout the Hundred Years' War in the 14th century and was all but destroyed in 1377. When the sea began to recede in the 15th and 16th centuries and the navigation of the Rother dried up, its port and trade fell away rapidly, despite an influx of Huguenot (French Protestant) refugees, and Rye settled, via a persistent, systematic attachment to smuggling, into provincial and romantic obscurity. It is now 2 miles from the sea and G K Chesterton called it a 'wonderful inland island, crowned with a town as with a citadel, like a hill in a medieval picture'.

Bounded on three sides by rivers, Rye is best explored on foot, especially through its historic centre which is called the Citadel. There are vestiges of the old fortifications, although the eastern side of the town was completely destroyed by erosion. Fragments of town walls can be identified, but the most impressive survivals are the **Ypres Tower**, a square, three storey medieval fortification dating from 1250 and the 14th century Landgate, one of four town gates, with two large drum towers and a fortified gateway. Another building that dominates the town is the large and imposing church of St Mary the Virgin, which has a memorably panoramic view from the top of its tower. Despite the attacks of the French, the Protestant Reformation and a clumsy re-design in 1883, it has enough features, including an ornate clock with a massive 18ft/5.4m free-swinging pendulum, to sustain a passing visit.

A level footpath (walk can be downloaded from the English Heritage website) leads across Walland Marsh to the east to **Camber Castle**, built by Henry VIII in 1538-9 as part of a system all along the South Coast to protect key harbours from raiding and invasion. It is open on weekend afternoons in summer and detailed times can be found on the English Heritage website. Nearby, **Camber Sands** are suitable for bathing among the dunes.

Nineteenth century Martello Towers, built to oppose Napoleonic invasion can be found in Romney Marsh and at Rye Harbour, while the Royal Military Canal, designed both as a fortification and as a means of transportation has a well-preserved path and contact with diverse wildlife. Other steeper walks can be undertaken along the sea cliffs to gain views of Romney Marsh and Pett Level. Here are the remains of a submerged forest (5000 years old and visible at low tide), as well as the wreck of HMS *Anne*, which was wrecked in 1690.

Near the Kent Border

Moving up the Rother valley, one comes to Bodiam and its castle. Within its wet moat, **Bodiam Castle** is the quintessential medieval castle, erected by Sir Edward Dalyngrigge in 1385 to help protect the area against French raids and invasion. It is square, with its corners and gates reinforced by towers and elaborate defensive measures and with the domestic and storage arrangements built against the inner walls. The gatehouse is three floors high and is, today, reached by a static bridge, but it was originally connected to the barbican by a drawbridge. At the time that the castle was built, the style of architecture and situation were the height of fashion and it appears that display might have been partly the motivation for its construction. Nevertheless, the various water defences – of which only the moat remains – would have prevented all but the most determined attack or siege.

Battle Abbey gatehouse

*The Novices Room below the Dormitory, **Battle Abbey***

Winchelsea Church

Two of the lanes by **Rye Church**

The castle passed through various families and was sold by its owner at the time of the Civil War to pay a heavy fine for being a Royalist. It fell into disuse and was partially dismantled. Luckily, in 1829, John ('Mad Jack') Fuller, a local worthy with something of a reputation, started to restore the castle and his work was continued by Baron Ashcombe and Lord Curzon, who bequeathed it to the National Trust on his death in 1925. Although the inside is ruinous, with much material taken away for building elsewhere, the plan of the interior can easily be seen, there are lots of intriguing features and there is plenty to explore. Children will enjoy it.

Visitors to Bodiam should also see St Giles' church, which, despite heavy restoration by the Victorians, dates from the 14th century and is in an evocative setting. Inside, there are some interesting brasses. Boating and cruising is available between Bodiam Castle and Newenden on the Kent and Sussex border and also down to Rye through the Weald on the navigable section of the river Rother.

Alternatively, visitors can take a steam and heritage diesel train for the 10½ miles/17km through the Rother Valley to Tenterden in the Kentish Weald. The **Kent and East Sussex Railway** operates trains that are usually hauled by steam locomotives, although some off-peak services are operated by diesel multiple units. At Tenterden Town station, there is the **Colonel Stephens Railway Museum,** as well as a gift shop – selling the inevitable Thomas the Tank Engine and other railway stuff – the Carriage and Wagon Department and a café that was once the Maidstone & District Motor Services Ltd Bus Station, moved from Maidstone. The 'missing link' between Bodiam and Robertsbridge is being rebuilt by volunteer members of the Kent and East Susssex Railway. To the east, **Northiam** is a picture-postcard village which has a beautiful 12th century parish church (St Mary's). At the top of the village and with a very tall spire, it is notable for its stained glass windows and fine tapestries. Nearby is the noted and unusual country house of **Great Dixter**. The original house at Dixter was a hall house dating from the mid-15th century, which was bought by a businessman, Nathaniel Lloyd, in 1909. Having discovered a condemned 16th century Wealden house of similar characteristics in Benenden (Kent), he had this house moved to Dixter. The two were combined through the incorporation of new work by the architect Edwin Lutyens, to create Great Dixter, which is a faithful reproduction of a medieval manor house and its internal arrangements, as seen through the romantic eyes of the Edwardians. Nathaniel Lloyd and Lutyens began the iconic garden at Great Dixter, work that was energetically taken on by Nathaniel's son Lloyd, Christopher the well known garden writer and television personality, until his death in 2006. The garden is in the arts and crafts style, and contains various distinctive elements: a series of grand cottage gardens, ponds, topiary, a Long Border, an orchard and a wild flower meadow. Lutyens designed the gardens as a series of rooms, incorporating pre-existing farm buildings and linking the house to the garden. This was continued by the Lloyds, but the overall approach has been one of bold experimentation and constant change and visitors are always impressed by the innovation and technical flair that the garden demonstrates.

Between Heathfield and Burwash, Bateman´s, built in 1634 by a local ironmaster, was the home of Rudyard Kipling from 1902 to his death in 1936. He and his family had moved from Rottingdean to escape the tourists who constantly peered through the windows of their double-fronted Georgian rectory, 'The Elms'. At 'Batemans', Kipling valued his privacy and, in the study that can be seen today, wrote *'If'*, *'The Glory of the Garden'* and *'Puck of Pook's Hill'*, in which the house, its setting and the wider local area feature prominently. This charming sandstone family house was given to the National Trust by his widow, with a garden designed by Kipling himself and contains many possessions and artefacts reflecting the author's interests and writings. There is also an interesting, working water mill and Kipling´s Rolls Royce. Kipling's local church – St Bartholomew's in **Burwash** – was originally built in the 11th Century and extended in the 1890s.

Just to the north and in the Wealden country on the border of Sussex and Kent, **Bewl Water** is south-east England's largest lake. It offers facilities for walking and cycling (cycles are available for hire),

including a 13mile/21km 'Round Water Route', water sports and angling, as well as the ability to cruise on a passenger boat amid wonderful scenery. Children can also enjoy a woodland adventure playground and rides.

Not far away is **Pashley Manor Gardens** – situated around a delightful Grade I listed timber-framed house, dating from 1550 and enlarged in 1720, the 11ac/4.5ha gardens are open from April to September and present an unbroken spectacle of design and colour. A winner of the Historic Houses Association/Christie's Garden of the Year Award, the landscaping is particularly effective, making good use of trees, sculpture and ponds to enhance the effect.

Another horticultural delight is **Merriments Gardens**, at Hurst Green, which was created the early 1990s to supplement the on-site nursery. Over 4 acres, there is a sequence of eye-catching garden designs likely to inspire the home gardener with their ingenuity, colour and variety and which incorporate plants available in the nursery. Highlights include the Golden Border, the Hot Border, the Ponds and Tropical Border and the Wild Area.

Close by, **Etchingham's** substantial Assumption of the Blessed Mary and St Nicholas Church began life in the 14th century as a private church for Sir William de Echyngham and had a moat. Its bells were forged in 1632.

Bodiam Castle

Herstmonceux Castle

Places to Visit

Batemans (NT)
Bateman's Lane Burwash Etchingham TN19 7DS
☎ 01435 882302
www.nationaltrust.org.uk/batemans
House open: mid-March to Oct daily Sat-Wed, 11am -5.30pm & weekends in Dec

Battle Abbey and 1066 Battlefield (EH)
Battle TN33 0AD
☎ 01424 775705
www.english-heritage.org.uk
Open: Apr-Sep, 10am-6pm; Oct-Mar 10am-4pm; closed 24-26 Dec & 1 Jan

Battle Museum of Local History
The Almonry High St Battle TN33 0EA
☎ 01424 775955
www.battlemuseum.org.uk
Open April-Oct Mon-Sat 10am-4.30pm Sun 12-3pm

Bexhill Museum
Egerton Road TN39 3HL
☎ 01424 787950
www.bexhillmuseum.co.uk
Open: Feb to mid-Dec, Tues-Fri 10am-5pm; Sat Sun & BH 11am-5pm

Bodiam Castle (NT)
Bodiam Near Robertsbridge TN32 5UA
☎ 01580 830196
www.nationaltrust.org.uk
Open: daily mid-Feb to Oct, 10.30am-5pm

Camber Castle (EH)
Harbour Road Rye TN31 7RS
☎ 01797 223862
www.english-heritage.co.uk
Open: July-Sept 2-5pm Sat, Sun and BH only

De la Warr Pavilion
Marina Bexhill on Sea TN40 1DA
☎ 01424 229100
www.dlwp.com

Open: Mon-Fri 10am-5pm & 10am-6pm Sat & Sun
See website for events & exhibition programme

Great Dixter House and Gardens
Great Dixter Northiam TN31 6PH
☎ 01797 252878
www.greatdixter.co.uk"
Open: Apr-Oct Tues-Sun & BH Mons, Gardens 11am-5pm & House 2-5pm

Hastings:

East Hill Lift
Rock a Nore Road TN34 3AR
☎ 01424 781040
Open: daily 10am-5.30pm in summer; 11am-4pm in winter

West Hill Lift
George Street TN34 3EG
☎ 01424 451113
Open: daily 10am-5.30pm in summer; 11am-4pm in winter

Blue Reef Aquarium
Rock-a-Nore Road Hastings TN34 3DW
☎ 01424 718776
www.underwaterworld-hastings.co.uk
Open: daily from 10am-4pm (5pm Mar-Oct)

Fisherman's Museum
5-6 Rock-a-Nore Road TN34 3DW
☎ 01424 461446
www.ohps.org.uk/fishermens_museum
Open: daily 10am-5pm April-Oct; 11am-4pm Nov-Mar; closed 25 Dec

Hastings Castle
Castle Hill Road West Hill TN34 3AR
☎ 01424 444412
www.1066country.com/Hastings/attractions/castle
Open: Easter-Oct daily 10am-5pm; (4pm in Oct) Mid-Feb to Easter, Sat & Sun 10am-4pm

Hastings Lifeboat Station & Visitor Centre

The Stade Old Town
☎ 01424 425502
www.lifeboat.org.uk
Open: 10am-4pm daily except Jan & Feb weekends only. Check notice boards for crew training

Hastings Museum & Art Gallery

Johns Place Bohemia Rd TN34 1ET
☎ 01424 451052
www.hmag.org.uk
Open: Apr-Sept Mon-Sat 10am--5pm, Sun 11am-5pm; Oct-Mar Mon-Fri 10am-4pm, Sat & Sun 11am-4pm

Old Town Hall Museum

High Street Old Town TN34 1EW
☎ 01424 451052
www.hmag.org.uk
Open: Apr-Sept Mon-Sat 10am-5pm, Sun 11am-5pm; Oct-Mar Mon-Fri 10am-4pm, Sat & Sun 11am-4pm

Shipwreck and Coastal Heritage Centre

Rock-a-Nore Road TN34 3DW
☎ 01424 437452
www.shipwreck-heritage.org.uk
Open: daily Apr-Sep 10am-5pm; Oct-Mar Sat & Sun & some weekdays 11am-4pm. Check in advance.

Smugglers Adventure

St Clements Caves Hastings TN343RG
www.smugglersadventure.co.uk
Open: Easter to Oct 10am-5pm; Oct-Easter 10am-4pm

Herstmonceux Castle & Gardens

Hailsham BN27 1RN
☎ 01323 833816
www.herstmonceux-castle.com
Open: Apr-Oct 10am-6pm.
Castle Tours available certain days only.

The Observatory Science Centre

(Former Royal Greenwich Observatory)
Herstmonceux Hailsham BN27 1RN
☎ 01323 832731
www.the-observatory.org
Open: daily Feb-Nov

Rye:

Lamb House

West St TN31 7ES
☎ 01580 762334
www.nationaltrust.org.uk/lambhouse
Open: mid-Mar to mid-Oct Thurs & Sat 2-6pm

Rye Art Gallery

107 High St Easton Rooms TN31 7JE
☎ 01797 222433
www.ryeartgallery.co.uk
Open: daily except Tues 10.30am-4pm; Sun 12-4pm, closed at lunchtime

Rye Castle Museum & Ypres Tower

3 East Street Rye TN31 7JY
☎ 01797 226768
www.ryemuseum.co.uk
Ypres Tower: open daily, 10.30am-5pm from April
Museum: open Mon, Thurs, Fri 2-5pm; Sat & Sun 10.30am-1pm & 2-5pm from April

Rye Heritage Centre

Rye Strand Quay Rye TN31 7AY
☎ 01797 226696
www.ryeheritage.co.uk
Open: daily Apr-Sept 10am-5pm; Oct-Mar 10am-4pm
Christmas opening times vary, please phone for details

Winchelsea Court Hall Museum

High St Winchelsea TN36 4EB
☎ 01797 226382
www.winchelseacourthallmuseum.co.uk
Open: May-Sep Tues-Sat & BH 10.30am-12.30pm & 2-5pm; Sun 2-5pm

Yesterday's World

89-90 High St Battle TN33 0AQ
☎ 01424 777226
www.yesterdaysworld.oc.uk
Open daily Jan-Mar 10am-4pm Apr-Oct
10am-5pm

COUNTRY PARKS AND GARDENS

Hastings Country Park

Off Fairlight Road Hastings TN35
☎ 01424 813225
www.hastings.gov.uk/hcp
Visitor Centre open most weekends,
10am-4pm in winter; 10am-5pm in
summer

Merriments Garden

Hurst Green TN19 7RA
☎ 01580 860666
www.merriments.co.uk
Shop and cafe open daily 9am-5pm
(Sun from 10.30). Gardens open Apr-
Autumn

Pashley Manor Gardens

Ticehurst TN5 7HE
☎ 01580 200888
www.pashleymanorgardens.com
Open: April-Sep, Tues-Sat & BH Mons
11am-5pm

RAILWAYS

Kent and East Sussex Railway and Colonel Stephens Railway Museum

Tenterden Town Station, Station Road,
Kent TN30 6HE
Sussex Stations at Northiam and Bodiam
☎ 01580 765155
www.kesr.org.uk
For timetable see website.
Museum open same days Apr-Oct

VISITOR INFORMATION CENTRES

Arundel

1-3 Crown Yard Mews, River Rd
BN18 9JW
☎ 01903 882268

Battle & Bexhill

Battle Abbey, Gatehouse TN33 0AD
☎ 01424 776789

Bognor Regis

Belmont St PO21 1BJ
☎ 01243 290337

Brighton

Royal Pavilion Shop
4-5 Pavilion Buildings BN1 1EE
☎ 0906 711 2255

Burgess Hill

96 Church Hill RH15 9AS
☎ 01444 238202

Chichester

The Old Fire Station Stone Street
TN17 3HF
☎ 01580 715984

Cranbrook

The Weald Information Centre
Old Fire Station, Stone St TN17 3HF

Crawley

County Mall RH10 1FB
☎ 01293 846971

Eastbourne

Cornfield Rd BN21 4QA
☎ 0871 663 0031

East Grinstead

Library Buildings West St
☎ 01342 410121

Hastings

Queens Square Priory Meadow
TN34 1QR
☎ 01424 451111

The Stade (by coach park)
Old Town TN34 1EZ
☎ 0845 274 1001

Herstmonceux

3 The Old Forge, Gardner St
☎ 01323 833961

Horsham

9 The Causeway RH12 1HE
☎ 01403 211611

Lewes

187 High St BN7 2DE
☎ 01273 483448

Littlehampton

Look & Sea Centre
61-63 Surrey St BN17 5AW
☎ 01903 721866

Midhurst

North St GU29
☎ 01730 817322

Petworth

Market Square GU28 0AF
☎ 01730 817322

Rye

4-5 Lion Street
☎ 01797 229049

Seaford

37 Church St BN25 1HG
☎ 01323 897426

Shoreham

Adur Civic Centre Ham Road BN43 6PR
☎ 01273 263000

Worthing

Chapel Road BN11 1HL
☎ 01903 221066

FARMERS MARKETS

Arundel

Town Square
3rd Sat in month, 9am-1pm

Battle

Abbey Green
3rd Sat in month, 9am-1pm

Bexhill

Parkhurst Methodist Hall,
Parkhurst Rd
4^{rth} Thurs in month, 9am-12noon

Brede

Village Hall Cackle St
Every Fri 10am - 12noon

Brighton & Hove

Ralli Hall next to Hove Station
1st Sun in month 10am - 2pm

Burgess Hill

Church Walk
2nd Thurs in month, 9am-2pm

Chichester

East St and North St
1st & 2nd Fri in month, 9am-2pm

Crowborough

Pine Grove Car Park
4th Sat in month, 9am-1pm

East Grinstead

High Street
1st & 3rd thurs in month, 9am-2pm

Ford

Ford Airfield
1st Sat in month, 7.30am-2pm

Hailsham

Hailsham Cattle Market Market St
2nd Sat in month, 9am-12.30pm

Hastings

Robertson St
2nd & 4th Thurs in month, 9am-2pm

Batemans, set in lovely grounds and now in the care of the National Trust

Haywards Heath

Orchards Shopping Centre
St Wilfrid's Way
2nd & 4th Thurs & 1st Sat in month,
9am-2pm

Heathfield

Co-op car park High St
3rd Sat in month, 9am-12.30pm

Brighton

Ralli Hall next to Hove Station
☎ 01273 734021/814369
1st Sun in month, 10am-4pm

Crowborough

All Saints, Old Church Hall, Chapel
Green
☎ 01892 664064/653083
Every Fri, 8.30am-11am

Lewes

Cliffe Pedestrian Precinct
☎ 01273 470900
1st Sat in month, 9am-1pm

Rye

Strand Quay
☎ 01797 280282
Wednesdays, 9am-1pm

Uckfield

Luxford car park
☎ 01825 760646
1st Sat in month, 9am-1pm

Battle

Battle Country Market
Memorial Hall, High St
Fri, 10-11.15am

Battle Farmers Market

Abbey Green
3rd Saturday monthly

Bexhill

Parkhurst Hall, Parkhurst Road
☎ 01424 222969
4th Thursday monthly

Horsham

Horsham Carfax
Every Sat 9am-4pm

Hove

George St.
4th Sat in month, 10am-3pm

Lewes

Cliffe Pedestrian Precinct
1st Sat in month, 9am-1pm

Midhurst

North St
4th Sat in alternate months
8.30am-1.30pm

Petworth

Golden Square
4th Saturday in alternates months
8.30am-1.30pm

Pulborough

Village Hall
Last Saturday in month 9am-12noon

Rye

Strand Quay
Every Wed 10am-1pm

Shoreham

East Street
2nd Sat in month, 9am-1pm

Steyning

High Street Car Park
1st Saturday monthly
9am-1pm

Uckfield

Luxford car park library way
☎ 01825 760646
1st Sat in month, 9am-1pm

Worthing

South Street Square
4th Sat month 9am-2pm

Getting there

Sussex is accesssible by rail from London Victoria, London Charing Cross and from London St Pancras via Ashford International. There is a frequent railway service along the south coast centred on Brighton.

The main north-south roads are: M23/A23 to Brighton, A29 to Bognor, A24 to Worthing, A26 to Lewes & Newhaven, A22 to Easbourne and A21 to Hastings.

The main east-west roads are: A272 from Uckfield to Petersfield and A27 from Eastbourne to Chichester.

London Garwick Airport is just north of Crawley adjacent to the M23

Beaches

Most of Sussex beaches are pebble ones but some have expanses of sand, especially at low tide.

Birling Gap
Bognor
Brighton West Beach
Camber Sands
Eastbourne - Falling Sands
Hove - Lawns
Littlehampton
West Wittering
Winchelsea

Cycling

East & West Sussex produce a series of leaflets and maps about cycling in the county. To download information access their respective websites: www.eastsussex.gov.uk & www.westsussex.gov.uk

SUSSEX FOOD AND DRINK

Sussex has a wide range of specialists producing high quality food and drink.
A comprehensive guide to producers can be found on: www.sussexfoodfinder.co.uk
Fish is landed straight off boats all along the Sussex coast at Rye, Hastings, Newhaven, Brighton, Shoreham and Littlehampton. There are numerous restaurants and cafés all along the coast serving fresh local fish and chips. Worthy of mention is the East Beach Café at Littlehampton. Two Sussex restaurants have Michelin stars – West Stoke House near Chichester and Ockenden Manor in Cuckfield.

There are eighty five cheese varieties made from cows', goats' or sheep milk with evocative names such as Sussex Blue, Sussex Slipcote, Sussex Crumble, Beacon Down, Five Ashes and Ashdown Forester. Local breweries are well represented as well. The oldest brewery in the county is Harvey's with up to 33 beer varieties including Sussex Best and in the west of the county, Ballards Brewery is renowned for beers such as Midhurst Mild and Nyewood Gold. More brewery information can be obtained on www.brightoncamra.org.uk/Breweries.html"

The chalky subsoil of Sussex is similar to the soil found in Champagne. Sussex vineyards produce award winning fine wines, including some exceptional sparkling wines which have been known to regularly beat French Champagne in international competitions! Many of the vineyards are open to the public for visits and tastings.

Vineyards to Visit

Barnsgate Manor Vineyard
Herons Ghyll Nr Uckfield TN22 4DB
www.barnsgate.co.uk
☎ 01825 713366

Bookers Vineyard
Foxhole Lane Bolney RH17 5NB
www.bookersvineyard.co.uk
☎ 01444 881575

Carr Taylor's Vineyard
Wheel Lane Westfield Hastings
TN35 4SG
www.carr-taylor.co.uk
☎ 01424 752501

Nyetimber Vineyard
Gay Street West Chiltington
RH20 2HH
www.nyetimber.com
☎ 01798 813989

Ridgeview Vineyard
Fragbarrow Lane
Ditchling Common BN6 8TP
www.ridgeview.co.uk
☎ 0845 345 7292

Sedlescombe Vineyard
Cripps Corner Sedlescombe
TN32 5SA
www.englishorganicwine.co.uk
☎ 0800 980 2884

Lurgashall Winery
Lurgashall GU28 9HA
www.lurgashall.co.uk
☎ 01428 707292

Useful Websites:

www.visiteastbourne.com
www.sussexbythesea.com
www.1066country.com
www.visitchichester.co.uk
www.visitworthing.co.uk
www.sussexmillsgroup.org.uk

Walking

The 101 mile long *South Downs Way* is the most famous of all the walking trails which go through the classic Downland of Sussex. Starting just east of Winchester in Hampshire, it finishes at Eastbourne.
For further information:
www.nationaltrail.co.uk/southdowns
and www.visitsouthdowns.com

Another national walking route (610 miles in total) which runs through Sussex is the *Monarch's Way* which follows the escape route taken by Charles II in 1651. The Sussex section runs from Rowlands Castle to Shoreham Harbour.

Other routes:

Centurion Way Railway Path - Chichester to West Dean – 5 miles
High Weald Landscape Trail – Horsham to Rye – 90 miles
Saxon Shore Way – Gravesend (Kent) to Hastings – 163 miles
Sussex Border Path - Thorney Island to Rye following the county border – 150 miles
Sussex Ouse Valley Way – Lower Beeding to Seaford Bay – 42 miles
Wealdway – Gravesend (Kent) to Eastbourne – 81 miles
West Sussex Literary Trail – Horsham to Chichester – 55 miles

Index

Index